THE POLITICS OF INDUSTRY

CHRISTOPHER HELM VITAL ISSUES SERIES
Series Editor: Geoffrey Alderman

Britain: A One-Party State?
Geoffrey Alderman

The Crisis of Unemployment
Alan Gordon

The Education Crisis
Norman Graves

Racism in Britain
Brian D. Jacobs

THE POLITICS OF INDUSTRY

Royce Logan Turner

CHRISTOPHER HELM
London

© 1989 Royce Logan Turner
Christopher Helm (Publishers) Ltd, Imperial House,
21–25 North Street, Bromley, Kent BR1 1SD

ISBN 0–7470–3215–7

A CIP catalogue record for this book
is available from the British Library

Typeset by Columns of Reading
Printed and bound in Great Britain by Billing and Sons Ltd, Worcester

Contents

Preface

This book is about the political environment within which business and industry operates. It examines the leading actors within that environment: governments, business itself, and trade unions. After examining the connection between business and politics, and different approaches to understanding that relationship—free market, and intervention and Marxist—it moves on to look at what has been one of the most important issues in post-Second World War political debate: the reason why Britain's economic and industrial performance was so poor for so long in relation to her comparable neighbours. The financial sector, cultural factors, mismanagement by governments and firms, and the role of trade unions are explained and analysed in this section.

The book then concentrates on a series of examinations of key areas in the political-industrial/business debate: nationalisation; privatisation; regional policy and the role of the 'Department for Enterprise'; the political and economic influence of multinational corporations; the debate surrounding the importance of high-tech industry and its promotion; the politics and effectiveness of small business promotion; the input of local authorities; the potential and actual input of the European Community; and an excursion into what the future might bring.

The final part focuses on two energy industries in Britain which, together, epitomise the old and the new: coal and nuclear power. The miners' strike of 1984/85, which, alongside the privatisation programme, was one of the most important events in the 'politics of industry' in the 1980s, is examined within, as are the arguments for and against nuclear power and the industrial performance record of the nuclear power industry in Britain.

The theme throughout is on the political. Economics, business affairs, industrial matters cannot be fully understood without making that recognition. The aim of this book is to be informative on the political-industrial/business debate and provide the reader with a framework for the understanding of some of the most vital issues of the late twentieth century.

For Sharon and Carlo

PART ONE
The Background

1. The Nature of Industry and Business

Industry has placed a series of key issues on the British political agenda over the post-war era. Indeed, little else has rivalled the prominence of the 'politics of industry' as a set of items of abiding newsworthiness. Its watchwords are legion, its ambit wide-ranging. Strikes, nationalisation, redundancies, closure, privatisation, profit-sharing, multinational investment, share-ownership, enterprise, skill shortages, unemployment; these represent just some of the terms that have dominated media coverage of the politics of industry, and provide part of its popular roll call.

The use of the term 'industry' is, in itself, often ambiguous and it is essential that the parameters of its meaning are defined at the outset. Most people's conception of 'industry', when the term is raised, comprises a notion of factories, coal mines, distribution services such as railways and lorries, power generation, quarries, production lines. The image conjured up is predominantly one of manual work, grease, machinery, overalls, noise. Yet others—and increasingly so as 'heavy' and manufacturing industry has declined—speak of the 'tourist industry' and the 'insurance industry' and, in more general terms, 'service industries'. Agriculture, too, is often termed an 'industry'—the food production industry—although most people, with a mental picture of pleasant green farmland, as opposed to the realities of factory farming and intensive crop production, fail to think of it like that. A lot is also heard of 'sunrise', 'sunset' and 'smokestack' industries. As a technique for maintaining readers' interest in a subject, the development of such terms is useful, although in practice the boundaries between 'sunrise', 'sunset' and 'smoke-stack' are often blurred. In the late 1970s and early 1980s, for example, the steel industry was almost universally seen as a sunset industry: an industry whose time had been and gone, upon which the industrial sun had set. In the late 1980s, the British Steel Corporation—the major producer of steel in Britain—was back in trading profit, and was once again seen as a company with a future. In 1988, it produced a trading profit of £410 million, the best result since the corporation was formed in 1967, making it the most profitable steel producer in Europe in that year. The turn-around in industrial productivity was equally dramatic. While it took 12 man hours to produce a ton of steel in 1980, in 1988 it took only 3.7.[1] Similarly, electricity generation by coal-fired power-stations has been seen as classic 'smokestack' industry: an emitter of pollutants which, in this case, are argued to have been a contributory factor to the acid rain which is said to have destroyed forests and buildings across a wide swathe of Europe. Yet the technology to diminish if not eliminate the emission of pollutants from coal-fired power-stations, thereby removing the smokestack nature of the industry, exists and has been applied in some cases.

The first lesson in the politics of industry, then, is that it is a dynamic politics, a politics subject to change and fluctuation. As in all politics, there are a few long-term certainties. In general, 'sunrise' is used to describe an industry which is reckoned to have prospects for growth, is relatively clean, and offers relatively good working conditions. The microchip industry is the classic sunrise industry. 'Sunset' is used to describe industries widely perceived to be obsolescent, industries of the past. Many sunset industries are also described as 'smokestack', that is, dirty, polluting, generally unpleasant. Coal-mining is often regarded as the quintessential smokestack and sunset industry, although there are strong grounds for arguing that that view is far too pessimistic, for the actual and potential uses of coal are enormous, ranging from the production of oil and gas through to chemical manufacture. It is probably too good a commodity simply to burn.

Industry here is defined in broad terms. It is a collection of activities—of humans and machines, of capital and labour—that *produce* goods and services. The production of goods and services requires inputs: of materials and information; of management in various degrees; of labour which carries out management-determined tasks—in which a small business might be performed by the management itself, which may consist of just one person. It requires a location. And the end product is an *output* of one sort or another: manufactured goods, other 'consumable' products, or services of one kind or another, of which entertainment, consultancy and education are just some examples.

This complex of activities takes place within an environment which is conditioned by *decisions*; decisions that are made at the political/governmental level and at the level of the organisation itself. How should increased profits be distributed? To increase dividends paid out to shareholders, or to increase the pay of the workers? How high should the taxes levied by central and local governments be? Will low taxes on companies encourage further productive investment or merely be syphoned off into increased conspicuous consumption by directors indulging in Porsches? What about trade union organisation? Should it be allowed by the Government? Should it be allowed by the company? Should just one union be allowed in the factory or several?

It becomes immediately obvious that there is a strong inter-relationship between the economic, political and social environment which government decision-making helps to provide and that which is created by the management of companies. The two worlds do not exist independently of each other.

NOTE

1. The *Guardian*, 9 June 1988; the *Independent*, 7 July 1988.

2. The 'Politics' of Industry

Government policies which affect industry need not be specifically targeted at it. Policies on housing, for example, affect industry because they affect the mobility of workers. In Britain in the 1980s, unemployed workers from parts of the north are precluded from finding work in buoyant parts of the south because they cannot afford the far more expensive housing there. Foreign and diplomatic policies also affect industry because they can affect trade and the extent to which foreign markets are open to British firms. Countries deeply involved in trade with, and investment in, white-run South Africa, for example, might well jeopardise their trade with black African states. Or a country such as Cuba, on the doorstep of the USA but with close political links with the Soviet bloc, jeopardises its industrial and trading connections with the USA because of those links.

Above all, industry exists, as we all do, in a *political* environment. Political environments change, and as they do, the prospects for, and conditions impinging upon, industry, change also. The outcome of elections, at both local and national level, for instance, have an immediate and long-term bearing on industry. Any prospect of a left-wing government assuming power in Britain, for instance, is likely to cause investors to remove their money, producing a fall in the level of the external value of the pound sterling. That means that more pounds have to be made available to buy foreign produce, which may cause domestic inflation as prices rise and wage claims are made to compensate for those rises.

Moreover, the contours of the politics of industry encompass a far wider territory within society than might at first appear. The Thatcher government's policy of encouraging wider ownership of shares, for instance, has important political repercussions. It was not long ago that share ownership was completely beyond the reach of the 'ordinary' man or woman; it was perceived as being something for a rich elite group of businessmen, most of whom lived in London. The industrial and economic policies of the Thatcher governments since 1979 have changed all that. A survey carried out by Dewe Rogerson, a City public relations firm, the results of which were published in August 1987, found that a quarter of Britain's adult population were shareholders: approximately 9.4 million people.[1]

Such newcomers to shareholding are susceptible to having their political persuasions modified by their newly acquired status. A political party which seems to represent a threat to that status, as the Labour Party appeared to in the general election campaigns of 1983 and 1987, can suffer electorally from this newly entrenched vested interest.

A similar example of the political ramifications of industrial changes concerns the decline of the manufacturing sector and the concomitant rise of the service sector. The century has witnessed an important change from a position where the majority of the population earned a living in manual occupations to one where most people now have white-collar jobs. The manufacturing economy has become the information economy. This industrial change has provided for the rise of a white-collar 'salariat'—rather than the old, working-class 'proletariat'—who no longer regard themselves as 'working class' in the traditional sense and who therefore owe less allegiance to political parties that have in the past been seen as defenders or supporters of the working class. In Britain, the party to suffer from these trends has, of course, been the Labour Party and the policy review under way in the late 1980s is in large part an acknowledgement of this.

This essay will concentrate primarily on the politics of industry with industry seen in its conventional sense: manufacturing, extractive, transport and distribution. It will examine how and why decisions are taken relating to industry; to what extent such decisions are ideologically as opposed to pragmatically arrived at; and how this affects all of us who live in British society. It will also focus on different assessments of why British industrial performance was so poor in relation to comparable countries, throughout the 1950s, 1960s, 1970s and early part of the 1980s. That performance *was* poor is not in serious dispute; for most of the post-war era, the right, the left, and the centre in British politics agreed on that if on little else. The evidence was readily available. Year after year, industry after industry contracted and lost orders overseas, and domestic markets were increasingly heavily penetrated by foreign companies.

What has been disputed is what to do about the problem, and this essay will also address itself to the competing approaches to overcoming it.

NOTE

1. The *Guardian*, 21 August 1987.

3. The Free Market Approach

At the outset it is as well to point out that there are competing theoretical and practical frameworks which can be constructed to accommodate government-industry relations. These differing frameworks are aligned, in different degree, to competing political parties. In turn, these differing frameworks are related to broader schools of economic thought.

The differing frameworks can also be seen as a typology of policy options in relation to government dealings with industry. Four such broad options can be identified. There is, first, the pure free-market approach; secondly, what has been called the 'social market' approach; thirdly, a policy of selective intervention, where governments intervene in various ways (by offering grants or loans as an incentive for a company to do something, for example, or threatening sanctions to achieve certain objectives) in a carefully targeted way, selecting certain companies or industrial sectors for attention; and fourthly an economy planned by Government, which might be akin to the Eastern European economies of the post-war era, and which might, by some, be called 'socialist'.

The pure free-market approach to industrial policy is associated with what is described as the school of liberal political economy. It proposes no intervention whatsoever by governments in the workings of industry, or indeed in any other area of the economy. The theory is that if everybody pursues their own selfish interests, such individual behaviour will aggregate to produce the greatest economic benefit to society as a whole. Any government intervention to correct a market weakness—for example, to try to induce a company to employ people it would not otherwise have done in a particular location—would simply have a degenerating effect on the economy as a whole and exacerbate the original problems.

The school of liberal political economy is associated with writers and philosophers such as Adam Smith, J.S. Mill, Ricardo and, in more modern times, Milton Friedman. Its origins lie in the classical political economy of the British and French schools, emerging with the writings of Smith and Ricardo. It involved from the outset a discussion of the principles upon which economic policy should be conducted. When economics of this kind first emerged in the eighteenth century (Adam Smith's famous book *The Wealth of Nations* was published in 1776) the economy was very different in nature from the late twentieth century. Industrialisation was just beginning, and the economy was still predominantly agricultural. It was not until the 1830s and 1840s that Britain had passed through the first stages of its transformation to an industrial economy.

The major thrust of the liberal political economic school was to emphasise the primacy of the free market in the economy. Whatever the outcomes of the free market in terms of the wealth of the people, economic efficiency and economic growth, they would be of the greatest benefit. Indeed, whatever the outcomes, they *had* to be accepted by people and governments. Debate within the school of liberal political economy was more or less confined to the kind of economic and social frameworks and principles within which a market-based economy could operate best. J.S. Mill summed up his view in the following terms:

> *Laissez-faire* should be the general rule: every departure from it, unless required by some great good, a certain evil.[1]

Moreover, liberal political economists did and still do, associate freedoms to buy and sell what one wishes within the market-based economy with political freedom. Milton Friedman, for example, in a critique of government intervention in the economy, has written:

> As consumers we are not even free to choose how to spend the part of our income that is left after taxes. We are not free to buy cyclamates or laetrile, and soon, perhaps, saccharin. Our physician is not free to prescribe many drugs for us that he may regard as the most effective for our ailments, even though the drugs may be widely available abroad. We are not free to buy an automobile without seat belts. . .You are not free to offer

your services as a lawyer, a physician, a dentist, a plumber, a barber, a mortician. . .without first getting a permit or a license from a government official. You are not free to work overtime at terms mutually agreeable to you and your employer, unless the terms conform to rules and regulations laid down by a government official. . .You are not free to set up a bank, go into the taxicab business. . .without first receiving permission from a government official. . .[2]

Friedman was writing in 1980 about the USA, of course, but his criticisms, right or wrong, could equally apply to Britain and most other advanced industrialised democracies.

Liberal political economists make certain assumptions which underpin their analysis and their economic prescriptions. First they assume that economic agents—in other words, people and firms—are fundamentally rational and well-informed about the different options open to them. They will then choose the course of action that benefits them most greatly. In real life, of course, neither full rationality nor full information can be taken for granted. Secondly, there is the assumption of egoism. Individuals are motivated, it is argued, by egoism in their economic and social activities. They will pursue self-interest; not only that, they *should* pursue self-interest because when the liberal political economy policy is followed within a given set of rules (a stable currency, laws which enforce contracts), then everybody will be free to follow, and hopefully fulfil, their own self-interest. A third assumption is freedom under the law. Individuals must be free to take their own decisions: what to buy, what to sell, what to offer as services to others. Friedman's advocacy of freedom confirms this. Most liberal political economists, however, accept that there should be some minimal restraints on individual behaviour. Most would be against legalising the trade in heroin, for instance. Most would be against legalising child pornography. This minimum is crucial if economic liberalism is to avoid becoming a form of right-wing anarchism.

Certain other assumptions are necessary if a liberal political economy is to work effectively. There has to be equality under the law, thus ruling out slavery. And, in order to organise exchange within the market, there has to be a stable currency, the value of which is not undermined by inflation. The phrase 'sound money' resonated through speeches and pronunciations on the economy in the Thatcher era of the 1980s, and it is for this reason. A market-based economy encourages countries and individuals to specialise in a narrower range of goods or services than might otherwise be the case. The 'law of comparative advantage', as it is known by economists, holds that this is a good thing for all. For example, a country particularly rich in coal reserves which can be cheaply mined and transported might seek to sell this to a country, or at least companies within a country, where coal is less plentiful and more expensive to mine. The second country, however, might have a highly developed financial sector able to provide cheap and efficient insurance policies to people in the first. Both countries are said to benefit from this interchange.

What happens alongside this, however, is that there is a tendency for any local self-sufficiency or national self-sufficiency in an economy to give way to an *interdependency* within the market. This is not necessarily a bad thing, but there are those who argue, for instance, that it is important to maintain a national self-sufficiency in energy production or defence equipment. And as an example of why, they would point to what happened to oil supplies to the west in the 1970s. Throughout the 1960s they had been cheap and plentiful; but during the 1970s the OPEC cartel flexed its muscles and inflicted increase after increase, with prices quadrupling in 1974 alone.

Within extreme versions of liberal political economy it can be argued that *everything* becomes a commodity, able to be bought and sold, traded in the market. Health care can be bought and sold in the same way as oranges in a market place. So can educational services although here there is the sobering thought that the private purchasing of education cannot guarantee achievement or scholarship.

Sexual services can also be bought and sold. Provided the individuals are acting of their own free will, and are aware of any health risks that might ensue from such activity, then there is no reason why sovereign individuals should not be allowed to form a market. It is sovereign individuals who make the choices and suffer, or benefit, from the consequences.

The emphasis placed on the market, and the right of sovereign individuals to make decisions within the market, is reinforced by the minimal role that liberal political economists see for the state. It has a role to play, but that role must be clearly defined and related to specific activities that others within society would be unwilling to perform: defence of the realm; policing; enforcing contracts; maintaining a stable currency. There is seen to be a clear boundary between the activities of the state and those of the rest of the economy. Beyond that boundary, there should be no transgression by the state. Part of the reason for the privatisation of nationalised industries by the Thatcher governments in the 1980s is that it was believed by them that the role of the state had grown too big; the boundaries had been transgressed. They needed, they felt, to withdraw from areas which should have nothing to do with government.

The school of liberal political economy insists on a strong state in order to guarantee free competition: a strong police force, a strong defence of the realm, a strong attitude towards enforcement of contracts, and a strong determination to defend the value of the currency. But this minimal state is not to interfere with the process of free competition or the outcomes of it. It exists to hold the ring while others fight it out for advantage. The state is also seen as a parasitical body: to continue to exist it depends upon contributions in taxes from the rest of us in society. This is another reason for wanting to keep the role of the state minimal. The bigger the role of the state, the more taxes have to be raised to finance it. Such taxes have to be levied on often hard-earned incomes; incomes which liberal political economists believe sovereign individuals should be able to spend as they wish. Excessive taxation is believed to impinge on freedom, to be a form of unacceptable coercion. Thus the policy implications of the school of liberal political economy are the free market, free trade, and the minimal state. In terms of policy towards industry this means allowing companies, businesses and individuals to be free of government ownership and interference. They should be allowed to get on and do what they want to do, and trade with whomever they wish in whatever commodities or services are legally permissible. Undoubtedly, the foundations of the Thatcher governments' policies towards industry and the economy in general since 1979 and through the 1980s are located within this school of thought.

As a political philosophy, and as a prescription for policy, liberal political economy has obvious attractions. It allows governments, for example, to absolve themselves from responsibility for many economic problems. If there is unemployment, for instance, governments can blame that on economic agents blocking the workings of the market economy; trade unions may be singled out as the culprits for excessive wage demands. Moreover, the emphasis placed on 'freedom' has an obvious appeal. Everybody, or almost everybody, is in favour of freedom. The problems arise, however, because 'freedom' means different things to different people. To liberal political economists it means freedom to buy and sell and offer services within the market. To others, it might mean freedom from poverty, or freedom to live in a clean, decent environment. It might mean the freedom provided by a sense of social security; to know, for example, that if one is homeless, shelter will be provided by public authorities.

Critics of the liberal political economy school of thought and the concomitant free-market, 'hands off' approach by some governments to industry and business, also stress the potential disadvantages of the strong emphasis on pursuing one's own self-interest so single-mindedly within the economy and society. Surely, they argue, such a stance is not far from encouraging greed and selfishness, and would breed intolerance in society? As one of the seven deadly sins, greed can hardly be considered a virtue. This was precisely the criticism made of the Thatcher government made by Roy Hattersley, Labour's deputy leader, in 1988. Secondly, argue critics, do not the areas in which intervention *is* deemed accceptable by liberal political economists set precedents for wider intervention in the economy? For example, if pensioners can be accorded subsidised travel permits, or Christmas bonuses, can this not be extended to the unemployed? Once it has spread to the unemployed can it not be extended to those on low incomes? And once this kind of spiral has started, where does it stop? It is not long before everybody, every industry and business can claim to be a 'special case'.

The major criticism of the liberal political economy school, however, is that it encourages and fosters great disparities between wealth and poverty, and allocates resources badly into the bargain. Because for all its slogans of equality under the law, it nevertheless remains a key concept within this view that money talks. Those who have money will be able to buy access to special educational or health-care services or find their way into jobs through family and financial contacts. The person from the poorer family will be denied access to this social ladder and yet it may be he or she who has the greatest potential to develop skills and thus benefit the economy in a particular area.

NOTES

1. Quoted in Carr.
2. Friedman and Friedman, p. 66.

4. The Social Market Approach

The second approach to industrial policy is the social market approach. 'Social market' is a phrase which has become quite fashionable in the 1980s, and yet its meaning remains obscure to most people. As is usual in politics, different people have used the term to mean different things. One meaning stresses that the extent to which a government allows a market to be free or otherwise has certain social effects, and that these should be taken account of by governments in determining policy. For example, the free market in housing has allowed prices to soar throughout the country in the 1980s, especially in the south-east and East Anglia. The 'social' effect of this is that more and more people, especially young people, are going to find that they cannot afford to purchase a house. The more commonly accepted meaning, however, is that the social market approach recognises the importance and efficacy of the free market as an economic tool, but also recognises that there will be areas where government intervention will be necessary. The country often regarded as a 'model' social market is post-war West Germany, the land, for a long time, of the miracle economic boom.

The approach is located within the liberal political economic school, stressing as it does the need for free markets, free trade and keeping any necessary government intervention to a minimum. The socialist cat, prone to intervention on a much wider scale, must be kept in the bag. If the Thatcher governments' policies towards industry and the economy in the 1980s can be characterised in a single term, that term is probably the social market approach. They have not been so generous as far as the social side is concerned, but there have been interventions within the market: subsidies to Rolls-Royce for aircraft engine development; tax relief and other incentives to small businesses; grants to inwardly investing multinationals like the Nissan car company which came to the north-east of England in the 1980s; subsidies to 'buy off' miners so that pit closures could take place more smoothly and the industry could be contracted with less disruption; subsidies to the railway, shipbuilding and steel industries to enable similar contraction; as well as subsidies to companies as incentives to introduce high-tech applications into their operations.

The social market approach also came to characterise the approach of Dr David Owen, one of the founders of the Social Democratic Party and leader of the continuing SDP in 1989, to industrial and economic policy, although admittedly his emphasis was different from Mrs Thatcher's. And so, for a whole swathe of the right and centre-right in British politics, the social market approach constituted part of the answer to the years of relatively poor industrial performance in Britain. The emphasis within this approach is laid upon the development of an economic climate in which business and industry is said to be able to flourish: an environment of lower taxes, more freedom for businessmen, and less red tape, bureaucracy and regulation. In the later 1980s, this strand of thinking was more finely developed by the Conservative government as they declared their intention time and again to shake off the 'dependency culture' of the past, where people were dependent on government for social security benefits and jobs and replace it with an 'enterprise culture'.

Indeed, central to the ideological analysis of Britain's economic difficulties over the post-war years presented by Mrs Thatcher and her governments in the 1980s is that the country lacked a significantly vigorous enterprise culture. Proponents of this thesis argue that, over the years, the entrepreneurial spirit has been in progressive decline in Britain. Businessmen, it is said, have behaved conservatively, and have been averse to taking risks and to innovation. They argue, furthermore, that the notion that one should sell one's labour to someone else, or some already existing commercial organisation, as opposed to establishing one's own business enterprise, has been too pervasive an ethos within British society. In a society in which an enterprise culture existed, these trends would be reversed. Entrepreneurship would be socially encouraged and the economic climate would be conducive to its success. Personal wealth would invoke admiration. Home- and share-ownership would be the norm. People would think more about setting up their own business rather than looking for a job. It was this understanding which underpinned Mrs Thatcher's vision that a future, robust economy would and should see, in her own words, 'every man a capitalist' and 'every man a man of property'.

Economics and politics are intertwined. Economics cannot, as John Maynard Keynes had hoped, become a technical, apolitical science something akin to dentistry. Economic and industrial policy prescriptions are applied, to a lesser or greater degree, with a political vision in mind. Sometimes the vision is blurred or vague, as it was, arguably, with the 1974–9 Labour government, and begins to correspond to a kind of 'muddling through', perhaps more kindly described as pragmatism. For others, the vision is clearer. For the Thatcher governments of the 1980s, the vision was crystal clear.

5. Government Intervention

The third approach to industrial policy can be called selective intervention. If a line can be drawn between pragmatism on one side and political vision on the other, this approach is closer to the pragmatic. It was the approach that was broadly followed in Britain between 1972 and 1979, and by Harold Wilson's earlier Labour government of 1964–70, and involves intervention by government at *selected* targets within the economy. Such intervention can therefore take various forms and can be located at various levels. It may involve intervention at the level of the individual company, or a particular sector within a larger industry—say the microprocessor sector within the larger electronics industry; or it may involve intervention by governments at an industry-wide level, as with Harold Wilson's decision to postpone 16 pit closures wanted by the then National Coal Board in 1967.[1]

The view of selective interventionists is that a government's macroeconomic management, by means of lowering or raising interest rates, lowering or raising general levels of taxation, attempting to set targets for the growth or level of the money supply, are insufficiently effective as a means of ensuring particular economic goals. Such goals may be, for instance, the maintenance or achievement of full employment or the avoidance of a balance of payments deficit. In other words, selective interventionists argue that macroeconomic measures need to be supplemented by other, more carefully targeted, policy 'tools', if all is to be well with the economy. These tools might include financial assistance in the way of loans or grants to a business or industry to enable it to produce a particular commodity or service, such as a high-tech application where the development costs are high and the returns from the project will not be received for some years. Alternatively, a government could use financial assistance to a company to try to get it to stop producing something or acting in a particular way. Financial assistance here might be seen as a 'positive' inducement, with the Government's alternative of imposing some kind of sanctions to achieve the same objective as a 'negative' inducement. A government might for example want to stop companies dealing with a country with which there has been a political or diplomatic disagreement; or it might like a company to stop producing say, weapons, and manufacture kidney dialysis machines instead. Dreams of such exchanges have entered the socialist lexicon under the terminology of 'socially useful production'.

Other tools of selective intervention might include taking into public ownership a particular company in an industrial sector; or setting up a new publicly owned company in a particular industry in order to provide greater competition, as happened with the creation of Girobank by Labour in 1968, or to provide greater government control, as happened with the setting up of the British National Oil Corporation by the 1974–9 Labour government. A government might also write off a company's debts in order to give it a new start, as the Conservative government did on the sale of the state-owned Rover Group to British Aerospace in 1988, when it made a direct cash payment of £547 million, and allowed for a further £500 million of debts to be written off against tax. It could also allow a company tax relief if it carries out certain product developments or locates in a particular area or behaves in some other way desired by the government.

The selective intervention approach to industry is associated with the wider school of economic thought dubbed the 'national political economy' school by the political scientist Professor Andrew Gamble in his book *Britain In Decline*. This school of economic thought grew up as a critique of the liberal political economy school. It is an eclectic school with eclectic foundations, drawing on Joseph Chamberlain's Social Imperialism movement of the early twentieth century which advocated tariff barriers on imports into the country and a British trading area based on the Empire; on the work of John Maynard Keynes who had criticised the analysis and assumptions of earlier free-market, free-trade economists; and more recent post-war economists such as John Kenneth Galbraith who also advocated active government intervention in the economy.

National political economy recognised that nations and states were units within the world economy, and emphasised these rather than the 'iron' laws of the market and the belief that decisions rested with sovereign individuals, argued by liberal political economists.

National political economy, though a disparate school, contained a core of central components. It pointed to the injustices that the unfettered free-market capitalism advocated by liberal political economists threw up: the extremes of wealth and poverty; the concentration of economic power in the hands of the few. It pointed to the booms and slumps in capitalism and the attendant social, political and economic problems that these presented. And it sought to emphasise that government *did* have the power to intervene in the economy and in markets to achieve certain ends: Keynes's great work in the 1930s for example was directed to showing what governments could do to counter the mass unemployment affecting Britain then.

A strong moral streak pervaded the national political economy critique of capitalism and the liberal political economy school: capitalism was obviously a system within which some prospered, and others went to the wall, and the vast majority in between earned a living but never became unduly prosperous. These moral criticisms remain in the 1980s with the Church of England criticising aspects of the Thatcher governments' economic policies. Indeed, revealingly, the controversially received Archbishop of Canterbury's Commission's report *Faith in the City* on conditions in Britain's urban areas was subtitled 'A Call For Action By Church And Nation'.[2] The Church of England, often dubbed 'The Conservative Party at prayer' was judged by some embarrassed Tories in the 1980s to be 'moving towards the left'.

Despite its criticisms of capitalism, the national political economy school never sought to abolish it. Far from it: Keynes felt that in the new post-war social conditions, capitalism was vulnerable as the deference of the working class had diminished, and as the attachment to the stabilising influences of the old society, such as religion, had declined. Essentially, Keynes feared for the continuation of civilisation and civilised behaviour. If the 'barbarians' were not kept happy with a more or less permanent economic boom, they might storm the barricades as they had done in Petrograd and Moscow, and bring to an end the English civilisation Keynes knew. As Robert Skidelsky notes:

> In the last resort Keynes's post-war fear for the future of capitalism was profoundly influenced by the Victorian fear of a godless society.[3]

The fourth approach to industrial policy regards the economy as in large part 'planned' by the Government and its agencies, with much greater public ownership of industry, and is associated with what can be called the Marxist school of political economy. The Marxist school views society and the economy in terms of class antagonism. As regards industry, their analysis points to an 'us and them' situation, with a mass of workers in a struggle against the employers as long as capitalism continues to exist. Thus while other schools of thought accept that there is at least *potential* for co-operation between workers in, and owners of, industry to achieve certain ends such as higher profitability, for Marxists this is simply a contradiction in terms. For central to the Marxist school of thought is this struggle between capital (or the owners of industry, land, businesses etc.) and labour (workers). This understanding coloured Marxists' attitudes towards a whole range of industrial matters in the 1970s and 1980s: moves towards industrial democracy under capitalism, for example, are seen as attempts to legitimise capitalism in the workers' eyes and therefore blunt assertive trade unionism and temper the urge for social transformation; no-strike deals by unions such as the EETPU are blatant 'class collaboration', a weak-kneed buckling to powerful employers at the expense of the rest of the working class; moves towards profit-sharing with employers in industry or other businesses are also seen as attempts to legitimise the capitalist system in the workers' eyes, a sort of 'buy off'; redundancy payments, too, are viewed as an attempt to defuse struggles against factory, plant, and pit closures. Arthur Scargill, President of the National Union of Mineworkers in the 1980s, and the most prominent Marxist trade unionist, has said the following of the industrial democracy procedures that obtained in the 1960s and 1970s in the coal industry while it was being run down:

> The consultation process [between the NUM and the NCB] helped to create an overall acceptance of the run-down and the 'free market' framework in which it occurred. The process of putting a particular pit in jeopardy involved consultation with the Area Union executive, rival reports by Union and Board mining engineers, and sometimes the setting of production targets. In this process, many NUM officials admitted to identifying with the outlook and aims of management. It is clear that consultation occurred on terms set by management and the Union found itself arguing on the same terms.

For Scargill, only assertive trade unionism, conceived of as part of the wider class war, could further miners' interests. Industrial democracy, even in this weak form of 'consultation', simply blunted that potential assertiveness.

Had the NUM taken industrial action in those years, many of the political decisions which destroyed the mining industry would have been reversed. The changes which did occur in the early 1970s were as a result of two national strikes in 1972 and 1974, which coincided with an increased demand for coal.[4]

NOTES

1. Hall (1981), p.81.
2. Archbishop of Canterbury's Commission on Urban Priority Areas.
3. Skidelsky, p. 403.
4. Scargill and Khan.

6. The Marxist View

Marxist political economy arose, of course, with Karl Marx himself in the nineteenth century, and it developed as a critique of the liberal political economy school. For Marx, the liberal political economy school failed in two ways. First, it assumed that there was a correlation between individual and general gain; by the individual pursuing self-interest, it was assumed that society as a whole would gain. Marx disputed this. For him and his followers, society remains a class society, in which the majority of people are systematically disadvantaged compared with a more or less permanent 'ruling class', which reproduces itself in its own image, whose individual actions are geared to suit themselves and their own class. The majority are effectively powerless.

Secondly, liberal political economy treated the development of free markets in the nineteenth century as the ultimate aim for which man had been struggling. The creation of the market was the ultimate end and the limit to what man could achieve. And therefore, if health care, for example, was not provided by rich philanthropists, then there would be no health care for those who could not afford it. If educational institutions were not established and maintained by rich philanthropists, then there would be no education for those who could not afford it. Indeed, more than a whiff of this—though it is not packaged as such—can be seen in the 1980s Thatcher government protestations that more money should come from the private sector towards health-care provision, education and inner-city redevelopment. But for Marx, this depressing picture of society was not good enough. He saw capitalism as another form of class-based society in which labour was exploited by the 'ruling class', and looked forward to a future, more 'happy' society, where exploitation and class were banished, which he calls in the *Communist Manifesto,* the 'communist society'.

In terms of industrial policy proposals, this school is the one most likely to argue that there is a need for *compulsion* by the state. The state, representing the interests of the majority, may need to *force* companies to do certain things. It may need to *force* banks to lend to industry. It may need to nationalise or take over the ownership of companies in order to exert control over the economy, or improve conditions for workers, or bring about greater economic equality.

Public ownership of industry, business and commerce plays a key role in the Marxist school. If society is exploitative, as they argue, then one means to remove that exploitation is to remove from the ruling class the *means* of exploitation: the ownership of industry and business. Once that is done, then power in society is not distributed in an uneven and inequitable way. We all become equally powerful, or powerless, depending on one's standpoint. And so Marxists and their allies have just as potent a political vision as the free-marketeers and liberal political economists: theirs is a happy land, with a heroic working class enjoying the fruits of their new-found equality and liberty.

This philosophical framework of liberal, national and Marxist political economy is by no means an abstraction from reality. It is, rather, the key to understanding much of what happens in the politics of industry, and the thinking behind the actions of many of the key actors in the field, be they politicians, trade unionists or businessmen. Most of the key movements in the politics of industry—privatisation, nationalisation, trade union developments —are related back to these philosophical underpinnings. In the run up to the nationalisation of the coal industry in Britain, for instance, in the 1940s, Will Lawther, the then right-of-centre President of the National Union of Mineworkers, could argue:

> What could be achieved through public ownership? It would win the complete confidence of the miners and their families. Generations of suspicion and hatred would be wiped out, and an entirely new attitude developed towards the coal industry. How can you run an industry efficiently, and get the best out of it, if every miner loathes his industry because of its owners; if every miner's wife swears 'her boy will not go down the pit'; if in every miner's home the pit is looked upon as an accursed thing?[1]

If there is a philosophical framework to the politics of industry, there is also an institutional framework. There are 'central actors' in British industrial politics, and those central actors are represented by different interest groups. Interest groups exist to pursue their interests and therefore they align themselves with political parties which they feel will try to promote those interests.

NOTE

1. Quoted in Heineman, Preface.

7. Central Actors in the Economy

The central actors in British industry are, obviously, those who own and manage it, and those who sell their labour to it. The chief interest group of the owners and managers is the Confederation of British Industry (CBI), but there are other important groups. The Institute of Directors, for example, is a collection of individuals, rather than being institutionally representative as the CBI is, and is a right-wing pressure group, actively campaigning for curbs on trade unions, cut-backs in the provision of services by the public sector, privatisation and the promotion of free markets. Then there is the City, whose interests are generally accepted to be represented by the Bank of England, which is, ironically enough, a state-owned institution. A host of other groups exist which represent and fight for the interests of the owners of industry and business: the Chemical Industries Association, the Society of Motor Manufacturers and Traders, the Engineering Employers' Federation, the National Engineering Construction Employers' Association, the National Farmers' Union to name but a few. Most large companies have their own public relations departments and will use them to represent themselves to governments or others they want to influence: GEC, for instance, one of Britain's largest manufacturing companies, is not even a member of the CBI. Unsurprisingly, these business groups feel more at home with the Conservative Party than any other, and it is business, effectively, which funds the party.

But the business community is not homogeneous in terms of its interests. A strong pound, for example, may please the City and industrial importers, for it cheapens the price of imports, but it may not please exporters, for it renders exports more expensive to the intended consumers. Nor do policies which suit big business always suit small business. Small shopkeepers, for example, might not welcome relaxations in the law which allow supermarkets to open on Sundays if the small shop does a lot of business then.

Those who sell their labour to industry and business, or a large number of them, form trade unions as their representative bodies. The basic idea of a trade union is that one individual worker standing alone against an employer is powerless, but where there is a unity of workers standing against an employer, their power is increased. In the words of the old maxim, unity is strength, and so the idea of having a Trades Union Congress (TUC) as a governing, umbrella organisation was to provide unity across the whole movement. In the 1980s, however, that unity appeared to be under considerable threat. 1988 saw the expulsion of the EETPU from the TUC for effectively flouting its authority over the signing of single-union, no-strike agreements. The miners, once considered to be the vanguard of the labour movement, remained split into two camps, the National Union of Mineworkers and the smaller rival, non-TUC Union of Democratic Mineworkers formed in and around the Nottinghamshire area after the strike of 1984–5. The Professional Association of Teachers was another no-strike, non-TUC union which grew in the 1980s. And for some time, there had been conspiratorial talk of a rival, non-socialist, alternative TUC.

Most (but not all) trade unions which are affiliated to the TUC are also affiliated to the Labour Party, and have traditionally looked to it to fulfil their aspirations. Indeed, the Labour Party was born out of the trade union movement at the beginning of the twentieth century.

Several problems arise from, and within, this relationship. First, it is argued by some that the close alignment of business with the Conservative Party and the trade unions with the Labour Party has exacerbated class antagonisms within the economy and society. Together with what is seen to be an unfair first-past-the-post electoral system which, it is argued, produces unrepresentative parliaments and governments, these intensified class antagonisms produce political parties which are constantly at each other's throats, are unable to work together or agree on anything and, when they achieve governmental office, repeal most of their predecessor's legislation. The ultimate loser is the country and the people, or at least so it is argued.

Secondly, in just the same way as the interests of the owners of industry and business are not homogeneous, neither are the interests of trade unions and different workforces. For example, in terms of energy policy, coal miners and nuclear power workers may have conflicting interests: if there is to be an increase in the amount of electricity generated, then it is in the interests of mining communities that this is produced from coal; it is in the interests of nuclear power workers that it is produced from uranium. It may be possible, of course, to compromise and satisfy both if demand for electricity is growing rapidly, but the fundamentals of the problem remain.

But the third problem is the most difficult to handle politically and practically. For a reasoned case can be made for saying that the Labour Party is in the hands of the trade unions, and the Conservatives lose no time in making it. Gleaning what one can from opinion polls in the 1980s, it seems that a number of the electorate agree and this cannot have helped in Labour's poor electoral performances in 1979, 1983 and 1987. The argument runs like this. The Labour Party, in different ways and at different levels, is in hock to the trade unions. They provide the vast majority of finance to the party, just under 80 per cent of the money raised at the national level. At the annual conference (formally the party's policy-making body) in 1988, for example, 89.26 per cent of the votes were wielded by the trade unions. Within the National Executive Committee, which is the policy-making body when the conference is not sitting, of the 25 members elected every year, 18 are decided by the union block vote. The electoral college which chooses the party leader and deputy leader accords the largest proportion of votes, 40 per cent, to the trade unions, with 30 per cent reserved for constituency Labour parties and 30 per cent for Labour MPs. In 1988, because of its size, the Transport and General Workers' Union alone held 8 per cent of the votes in the electoral college. Even in the selection of parliamentary candidiates, and therefore MPs, the power of the unions is entrenched by another 'electoral college', and in some cases their power is dominant. Indeed, in some constituencies it has been one union which has held overwhelming power in selecting parliamentary candidates, for example the NUM in certain seats in South Yorkshire, and the Transport and General Workers' Union in certain seats in the north-west of England. The problem with this, of course, is that were Labour to form another government, there would be accusations that it was not an independent force. Opponents of Labour would argue, moreover, that were it necessary for a Labour government to pursue a policy unpopular with the trade unions, or some trade unions, it would be unable to do so. And in that sense it is argued that Labour cannot govern the country with proper effectiveness: it is forever consulting unrepresentative trade union barons and where they disagree with a policy then the policy is dropped. That, at least, is the caricature. A further criticism is that where trade union leaders *do* consult their members as to how to exert their influence—for example, how to vote in the electoral college in a leadership election—then people who are *not* members of the Labour Party, indeed people who may be members of a different political party such as the Conservatives or the Communists, are exerting an influence over Labour Party policy. Even where consultation is restricted to members who pay the political levy in the union, these may not be committed Labour supporters.

The assertion that a political party is not an autonomous force and is instead operating at the behest of some interest group or other could also be, and frequently is, levelled at the Conservatives as well, in relation to business groups. After all, business finances the Conservatives and many leading Conservatives also run businesses or are company directors. But the connection is less obvious to the ordinary man or woman in the street. Adept at the art of politics and government, the Conservatives are more subtle about their connections. One does not see a procession of leading industrialists and businessmen trooping into No.10 Downing Street for beer and sandwiches—or, perhaps, in their case, claret and salmon. Of course, the Conservatives *do* consult leading industrialists and businessmen; the Thatcher governments of the 1980s did it frequently. It is just that the Conservatives are more subtle about it. Consultation is smoother, less obtrusive. The abiding, though perhaps exaggerated, memory of the 1970s and the Labour government of 1974–9 is of union leaders coming to No.10 with the country at crisis point over strikes, incomes policy, or the external value of the pound. The art of government is to make the sailing of the ship *appear* smooth even when it is not; the captain must *appear* to be in control even if his ship is really rudderless. With anything less, people lose confidence in the Government.

There are few places in the 1980s where all these 'central actors' in the economy—government, trade unions and top industrialists and businessmen—meet. The major institutional forum that remains is the National Economic Development Council, a tripartite body formed in 1962, which in the late 1980s, after scaling down by the Thatcher government, meets only four times a year. While its founders, Harold Macmillan's earlier Conservative government, had high hopes for it, it really only ever functioned as a talking shop. It is clear that the Thatcher government attaches little importance to it. And, given their political and economic philosophy, there is little reason why they should. For them, it is necessary that managements have the right to manage, and decisions affecting industry and business will therefore be taken by individual businessmen within the context of a free market. There is no role for trade union 'barons' to exercise a veto over such decisions, or to demand a set of concessions, and the only role for government is to ensure that an economic environment is provided within which industrial and business enterprise can flourish.

PART TWO
Explanations of Decline

8. Cultural Explanations

If the post-war record of British industry was for so long so bad compared with comparable neighbours, then there ought to be some attempt to examine the competing theories that have been put forward as explanations for this. Not all can be examined for they are numerous, and they range from blaming Britain's imperial past to blaming the electoral system. But a number of the major schools of thought can be addressed.

The notion that there are cultural factors which have had a tendency to provide for poor economic and industrial performance in Britain is one of the most intrinsically interesting, and is associated with a number of writers including the Marxist Perry Anderson, Tom Nairn, Martin Wiener and others. None of these writers, of course, provides exactly the same thesis; but what is common to them is that they point to a 'cultural exceptionalism' that has affected and afflicted Britain *vis-à-vis* other comparable countries such as Germany and France. Anderson, in 'The Origins of the Present Crisis', published in the Marxist periodical *New Left Review* (1964) held that the old, aristocratic, landed gentry had survived the industrial revolution of the nineteenth century and assimilated into its ranks the new industrial bourgeoisie—the owners of the new industry. By this process, in Marxist terms, the newly emergent working class was deprived of its 'natural enemy' and was therefore unable to formulate its own political vision of socialism. Similarly, the new industrial bourgeoisie, because they were unable to wrest power from the aristocratic landed class, failed to fashion a state with political institutions which would be conducive to industrial progress. In Anderson's own terms:

> In England, the whole cumulative tradition of the governing class disables it from this role: its virtues have been those of the agrarian squirearchy and industrial *laissez-faire*. Now that these are gone, only its vices are left: universal dilettantism and anachronistic economic liberalism.[1]

Martin Wiener, in his book *English Culture and the Decline of the Industrial Spirit 1850–1980*, also argued that poor economic performance in Britain has been connected with the survival of a culture which emphasises pre-industrial values. There are two key points in Wiener's thesis. First, the values held by the dominant social elite in England, and therefore Britain, given that England is the largest component nation of Britain, tend to permeate the wider society and therefore provide the basis for national values. Secondly, the transition to a modern, industrialised economy was in Britain achieved fairly smoothly, from within the country, rather than being the consequence of war or invasion, and thus disrupted traditional patterns of social behaviour, the class structure, values and political institutions far less than was the case in other countries. So, whereas in other countries, industrialisation had been brought about by new economic forces which irredeemably changed the nature of society—in the USA, immigration and civil war; in France, revolution, invasion and frequently modified political institutions; in Germany, near proletarian revolution, fascism and eventual bisection; in Italy, workers' rebellions in the 1920s; in Japan, the Second World War and the flattening of Hiroshima and Nagasaki by atomic bombs—in Britain there was more of an accommodation between the old, aristocratic, landed gentry and the new owners of industry, or industrial bourgeoisie. According to Wiener, this had a self-limiting effect for economic performance and industrial progress in Britain.

Britain was the world's first industrialised country. Yet, if Wiener is to be believed, it never had a straightforwardly industrial or bourgeois elite. The landed, pre-industrial aristocracy in Britain retained its cultural dominance and succeeded in fashioning the emergent industrial bourgeoisie of the nineteenth century in its own image. The consequences of this were that the rural was always considered superior and to be revered above the industrial; industrialisation was regarded as being ugly and something of an evil; and, because of these factors, the industrialist himself was never accorded a high status within society. In fact, what the industrialist himself came to aspire to, according to this argument, was the cultivation of the image of the 'country gentleman' with all its connotations of the pursuit of leisure and the cultivation of a gentlemanly style. Wiener asserts that through these social mechanisms, the zeal for inventiveness, money making and work subsided; while the ideal of becoming a 'gentleman' gained prominence. Even the modern industrial town would be abandoned by the industrialist as a place to live. Instead he would prefer a rural, preferably historic, home in emulation of the aristocracy. Wiener also lists a whole host of political leaders, writers, economists and other prominent figures who exuded and exalted this anti-industrialist style: people such as Stanley Baldwin, three times Conservative prime minister between 1923 and 1937; Nye Bevan, the respected Labour left-winger who presided over the establishment of the National Health Service in the Labour government of 1945; Ramsay MacDonald, the first Labour prime minister of Britain in 1924 and 1929–31, and then National Coalition prime minister between 1931 and 1935; George Lansbury, the Labour party leader between 1931 and 1935; Oswald Mosley; Quintin Hogg and Enoch Powell. The collective psyche was imbued with an anti-industrial ethos. The economists he mentions who imparted a suspicion of industrialism and material values range from J.S. Mill through to Keynes who worked and wrote primarily in the 1920s, 1930s and 1940s; Fritz Schumacher, who in his famous book *Small is Beautiful*, published in 1974, questioned materialistic values and argued that large-scale industry was often destructive to the environment, as well as being inappropriate to vast sectors of the world; and Professor E.J. Mishan, who was perhaps most notable for questioning the value of economic growth in the 1960s.

Architectural styles and the writings of well-read historians who dwelled upon this aristocratic, rural past also reinforced this culture. For Wiener, the English culture became a social force. He cites the cautious terms upon which the Conservative party accepted the industrial revolution as evidenced by the failure of Joseph Chamberlain, a Liberal Unionist who formed a coalition with the Conservatives in the early twentieth century, to capture control of the Conservative party on a platform of tariff imposition. Chamberlain, with his close associations with Birmingham, offered an urban, interventionist and industrial version of Conservatism but failed to get his ideas implemented. Instead, there was a gentry counter-revolution against industrial capitalism. The political elite, like the social and cultural elite of which it was part, desired but feared economic growth and industrial progress.

Criticisms of the Wiener thesis can be made, of course, and Wiener himself acknowledges some of these and attempts to answer them. For a start, his argument is open to the criticism that an agricultural and rural hegemony also persisted in nineteenth-century Germany, and Germany has been, in industrial terms, a far more successful country than Britain since the Second World War. He defends his thesis, however, by arguing that:

> Because the industrial revolution in Germany took place later and more suddenly than it did in Britain, the German bourgeoisie had less time to become accepted by and absorbed into the older elite. Second, the Prussian aristocracy [the *Junker*], in particular, was less ready than the English aristocracy to accept wealthy businessmen into its ranks, regardless of how much they hastened to remake themselves on the *Junker* model.
> . . .Moreover, the *Junkers*, for all their caste pride, were not wealthy on the English scale, and had to continue to struggle ruthlessly to protect and develop their economic and political position. . .
> In Germany, thus, capitalism and liberalism were devalued far more than industrialism, whereas in England it was industrialism and not capitalism or liberalism whose development was inhibited.[2]

There were other ways, Wiener argues, in which this anti-industrial culture was fostered in England. First of all there was the public school. The public school as an institution was culpable in itself, for it eschewed the teaching of science and instead concentrated on a liberal and arts curriculum and on the production of 'gentlemen'. But it was also culpable as an institution because the far more numerous grammar schools which followed looked to public schools for their model of education. Public schools provided, and arguably still do provide, in the late twentieth century, the formative experience of the English elite. Vocational training within them was frowned upon.

Grammar schools provided education for people several rungs down the ladder, but the people who attended them were, nevertheless, considered to be of higher intellectual calibre than others, even though the selection process for grammar schools took place at the very early age of ten or eleven.

The children of businessmen were not originally welcomed at public schools. And when they were allowed in later they were equipped with a training which would be more suitable for a life in public service than industry.

In a similar fashion to the public schools, the later Victorian Universities of Oxford and Cambridge also provided a common formative experience for the English elite. And again, according to Wiener, the values they inculcated centred on the desirability of pursuing the social role of the 'gentleman', and training for a career in public service rather than industry. The civic universities, such as Birmingham, Liverpool, Bradford, Manchester, Sheffield, Leeds and London, were different, for they did set out to provide a more practical education; but their problem was that they never threw off their inferior status *vis-à-vis* Oxford and Cambridge. Most businessmen throughout the nineteenth and twentieth centuries continued to aspire to an Oxbridge education for their children and, in this way, there was a 'haemorrhage' of business talent from the economy. By contrast, in neither of Britain's great industrial rivals, the USA and Germany, did the education system encourage a retreat from the industrial world.

C. Lorenz, writing on the subject in the *Financial Times* in 1982, put forward the view that:

> Technical education was eventually developed [in Britain], but specifically for the working class. With self-made manufacturers resisting the continental notion that education was an important factor in managerial success, technical education became irrevocably identified with the skills of the artisan.
>
> In Germany, by contrast, an elaborate set of state education at both secondary and university level, and embracing both classical and practical subjects, had been founded in Prussia in the early 19th century in the wake of a humiliating defeat at the hands of Napoleon; the system was quickly emulated by other German states.
>
> Not only was it socially acceptable for a well brought up lad to get a degree in a technical subject, but many such people went on to lead Germany's own industrialization, putting it at the forefront of innovative industries like chemicals and helping forge the basis for the country's continued industrial success in the twentieth century.[3]

As for attempts to reform the education system in Britain—comprehensivisation of schools in the 1960s and 1970s, the growth of polytechnics in the higher education system since the 1960s—Lorenz argues that many comprehensives developed a 'liberal', and therefore anti-technical, bias in the curriculum, and that many polytechnics have pursued liberal and arts-studies in order to attract 'better' students from the university sector. The city technology colleges (CTCs) being introduced in the third term of the Thatcher government are a recognition that the modern Conservative party accepts, at least in part, the drift of some of the above arguments on the absence of technically oriented education in Britain. It would fail to agree with the class-based substance of Wiener's and Anderson's analyses, however, preferring the 'it is individuals which do things' stance.

Associated with the above process, Wiener notes the rise of professionals throughout the nineteenth and twentieth centuries. By the second half of the nineteenth century, there were enough public officials, journalists, lawyers, doctors, dentists and other professionals to be considered a class in themselves. This represented a further drain of potential talent from industry and reflected the educational bias noted earlier.

A further problem that Wiener argues contributed to Britain's industrial debilitation relates to the series of financial institutions that are collectively termed the City, and their aloofness from British industry. First, the City was internationally oriented, and therefore did not, indeed does not, depend on a healthy British economy for its own health. Secondly, because of its proximity to the heart of upper-class England, its centuries-old history, and its ties with the aristocracy and gentry (dukes and duchesses are still 'names' at Lloyds in the 1980s), it always enjoyed a social esteem that eluded industry. Thus, for both cultural and economic reasons, a good deal of talent would be drawn to the City and, consequently, away from industry.

At a general level, Wiener's thesis can be criticised because it appears not to recognise adequately that it is possible for people to talk about, and admire, the countryside and rural values yet still be industrious. Secondly, one company Wiener criticises for having a 'gentlemanly' ethos in its management is ICI. And, although Wiener questions its marketing ability, the fact remains that ICI is one of Britain's most successful companies in the 1980s, and has been over the whole post-war era. In particular, it has expanded abroad by setting up production plants overseas.

Wiener cites Stanley Baldwin a lot, and Baldwin, with his tweed suits and frequent orations about English rural life, undoubtedly portrayed the image of the countryman. Roy Jenkins quotes one speech in which Baldwin spoke of

> the sounds of England, the tinkle of the hammer on the anvil in the country smithy, the corncrake on a dewy morning, the sound of the scythe against the whetstone, and the sight of a plough team coming over the brow of a hill, the sight that has been seen in England since England was a land, and may be seen in England long after the Empire has perished and every works in England has ceased to function. For centuries, the one eternal sight of England.[4]

But of course it was under Baldwin that the Electricity (Supply) Act of 1926 was passed which provided for the setting up of the Central Electricity Board which, over the next ten years, laid the national grid—an important spur to industrialisation in Britain. Moreover, it was under Baldwin's reign that the dominance of traditional rural life came to an end. By the time his period as Prime Minister had finished, the motor car and suburbia had become the twin symbols of a new social era.

A more empirical criticism is provided by Fiddler, who in a

survey of business elites in Britain published in 1981, found that 42 per cent of chief executives had higher education qualifications which included substantial economic or financial training; a further 21 per cent had science or engineering qualifications. This deals a severe blow to the argument that British business is run by people with non-relevant degrees. Economic and financial qualifications do not preclude incompetence, of course, but they do indicate that the right to wear a particular old school tie is not sufficient qualification to join British management.

Wiener's thesis is essentially a class-based analysis, and is therefore linked to the broader school of Marxist political economy mentioned earlier. Perry Anderson, one of Wiener's intellectual 'allies' and an author he refers to, noted in *New Left Review* in 1968 that:

> The class which accomplished the titanic technical explosion of the Industrial Revolution never achieved a political or social revolution in England. It was checked by a prior capitalist class, the agrarian aristocracy which had matured in the eighteenth century, and controlled a State formed in its image.[5]

Anderson goes on to say that these factors prevented a revolutionary left-wing culture from emerging in Britain: because the industrial bourgeoisie were politically subordinate, the industrial working class had no 'role model' to follow in the quest for political power. That may or may not be the case (but if it is the case why has a revolutionary left culture not triumphed in France, Belgium or Germany?), but for Wiener what it did do was to prevent industrial progress from going beyond a certain point. Liberal political economists would dismiss this as nonsense. For them, it is *individuals* that are the innovators and entrepreneurs, the active souls who, in the immortal words of a White Paper published in 1988 by the Department of Trade and Industry, 'make things happen'.[6]

These people do not see themselves as part of a social class, they are simply individuals who have energy and ideas. Of course, they may indeed *be* part of a social class—a class which has access to money and contacts which provide ideas and support for business ventures—but liberal political economists are keen to stress that, in their conception of a capitalist society, it is possible to start with nothing and still 'make it'. The 'rags to riches' story provides an important part of their vision.

NOTES

1. Anderson (1964).
2. Wiener, p. 9.

3. The *Financial Times*, 15 September 1982.
4. Quoted in Jenkins, p. 31.
5. Anderson (1968).
6. Department of Trade and Industry, Cmnd 278, p ii.

9. Mismanagement by Governments

A large section of intellectual opinion has argued that it is mismanagement of the British economy that has been the root cause of poor industrial and economic performance. Different writers stress different aspects of government policy: some have blamed the Treasury for traditionally pursuing policies aimed at ensuring a high external value for sterling; others, governments in general for behaving as if Britain was still a world power, keeping a large defence budget and military commitments it can ill afford, and again, defending the high level of sterling's external value. But a highly influential thesis which emerged in the 1970s was contained in a book published in 1978 by Robert Bacon and Walter Eltis and called *Britain's Economic Problem: Too Few Producers*.

That Bacon and Eltis's theories were accorded some importance by the Thatcher governments of the 1980s is attested to by the fact that Walter Eltis was appointed Chairman of the National Economic Development Office, taking over the job in November 1988.

Bacon and Eltis's thesis is fairly straightforward. The central point they make is that, beginning in the 1960s and continuing into the 1970s, there had been a steady and progressive increase in the number of people working in what they call the 'non-marketed sector'. The non-marketed sector they describe as being that sector which provides services which are not sold, but are paid for by the taxpayer: services such as health care, social welfare, education, local government services, central government service and quango services. Obviously the expansion which took place was in the public sector.

They seek to draw a clear distinction between the non-marketed and marketed sectors of the economy; this, they believe, is more useful than drawing a distinction between the industrial and non-industrial, which are narrower categorisations.

> Instead of dividing economic activities into those that are *industrial* and those that are *non-industrial* they can be divided instead between those that produce *marketed* outputs and those which do not. Almost everything that industry produces is *marketed*, that is, it is sold to someone. The private sector services are sold, so they are *marketed*. Defence, on the other hand, is not marketed; no one pays for the use of a regiment or frigate. What the National Health Service provides, and most schools, is also not marketed, and the services provided by policemen and civil servants are not marketed; so they must spend their incomes on the marketed products of the rest of the community.[1]

In sum, the deleterious effects of this increase were that labour was increasingly being drawn to employment in the non-marketed sector causing a lack of labour resources for the marketed sector and, in particular, industry; this in turn meant that a greater number of 'non-producers' were seeking to buy the products of a smaller number of 'producers', which might cause balance of payments problems if consumers sought to satisfy demand by buying foreign products; or inflation, as excess demand for domestically produced goods bid up their prices. In addition, the increase in taxes necessary to pay for the increased number of people employed in the non-marketed sector was further debilitating to the economy, reducing incentives to work hard, as a good proportion of the increased earnings from harder work would be taxed away. According to Bacon and Eltis, this shift in the use of labour resources was unmatched in its extent in any other country.

They state that:

> It is beginning to be appreciated that a very great structural shift in employment occurred in the British economy since about 1961, and this can be looked at in several ways. Perhaps the most significant is that employment outside industry increased by over 40 per cent relative to employment in industry from 1961 to 1975 and that this increase was most rapid in the public sector.[2]

Moreover, they blame political expediency for the problem;

politicians had been meddling with the economy for their own ends, and the end results had been damaging.

The increase in employment to produce more public services continued through boom and recession, and until 1975, each increase was permanent; so the workers taken on in recession were not available to industry in subsequent booms. There was, therefore, a kind of ratchet effect, with employment in health and education rising and never falling.[3]

It was seen as astute by politicians to improve social services; increasing public sector employment was easily achievable, and therefore could be used as a means both of maintaining full employment and of satisfying the demand for social, health and educational services. In the climate of the times, it would have appeared mean and unfashionable had the Treasury, or anybody else, sought to thwart plans for expansion by the Departments of Health, the Environment or Education.

There is a correlation between the analysis and policy prescriptions of Bacon and Eltis in 1978 and the later policies of the Thatcher governments: the emphasis on cutting back the public sector; on reducing taxation; on withdrawing subsidies from industry (for subsidies to industry effectively transfer production from the marketed to the non-marketed sectors and exacerbate the problems Bacon and Eltis referred to); and on transferring activities from the non-marketed sector to the marketed. This last policy means charging for activities previously funded by the taxpayer, as with the decision in November 1988 to charge for eye and dental check-ups, increased prescription charges in the Thatcher years, proposals to charge for stays in hospital, and so on.

Bacon and Eltis also argue that industrial investment in Britain did not take place at a sufficient level and this, too, was one of the key economic problems. This happened for various reasons. First, a great deal of money that might otherwise have gone into industry instead went into property in the 1970s, particularly after the Conservative chancellor Anthony Barber's reflationary budget of 1972. Times were inflationary, with assertive trade unionism and rapidly increasing commodity prices, and investors saw property speculation, in the context of rapidly rising property prices, as their best hedge against inflation. Secondly, according to the thesis, at the time trade unions were much stronger, better organised and more assertive in the industrial sector than they were in the services sector: this also militated against investment in industry. Thirdly, the authors pointed out that there is a lag between the point at which an economy is boosted by, say, a lowering of taxation or a fall in interest rates, and the point at which industrialists will invest to meet the resultant upsurge in consumer and/or industrial demand. During that lag, the public services sector pre-empted the labour power that was available, leaving insufficient for industry and the required industrial investment therefore never took place.

The argument of Bacon and Eltis is interesting, but not unchallengeable. It is, first of all, open to the criticism that it lays too much emphasis on what governments did at the level of macroeconomic management, and too little on micro-level problems: in other words, the individual marketing strategies of firms; the design and quality of the products themselves; the competence of British management. All these micro-level factors must surely be important. After all, if the policy decisions of governments were so bad, how was it that there were any industrial successes at all? Secondly, except for 1950 and part of 1951, Britain was governed by the Conservatives throughout the 1950s: any increase in the size of the public service sector was modest, and yet, clearly, Britain's relative industrial decline had already commenced then.

Other critics of the thesis might well point to Sweden, where the post-war era has seen prolonged periods of social democratic rule and a consequent growth in the non-marketed sector at least equal to Britain's, yet Sweden was a very successful economy over the period. A counter argument to this might be to say that Sweden is a much smaller economy than Britain and therefore direct comparisons might not be completely appropriate. Alec Cairncross, writing in a book edited by F. Blackaby called *De-Industrialisation*, argued that the Bacon and Eltis thesis flew in the face of the evidence to suggest a substantial *increase* in the volume of manufacturing investment—investment in the marketed sector—in the 1960s. A further claim by Bacon and Eltis was that the increase in the non-marketed sector had reduced exports, in other words, more of Britain's home production had gone to meet home demand. Karel Williams *et al* note, to the contrary, that:

> The British manufacturing sector is increasingly heavily committed to export business which accounted for 20 per cent of UK manufacturing sales in the mid-1950s and over 30 per cent by 1980.[4]

Nevertheless, the Bacon and Eltis thesis has been influential; and, for a variety of reasons, their emphasis on cutting back the non-marketed sector has found a welcome within the Conservative party of the 1980s. Undoubtedly, however, this welcome has more to do with political ideology than a watertight, politically neutral economic theory. This point will be discussed further in the later section on Privatisation.

NOTES

1. Bacon and Eltis, p. 27.
2. Bacon and Eltis, p. 12.
3. Bacon and Eltis, p. 15.
4. Williams *et al*, p. 3.

10. Mismanagement by Firms

If governments can get things wrong as well as right, in terms of economic policy, then companies and firms also take decisions which affect them for better or for worse. Such decisions, taken all the time by companies' managements, relate to a whole host of issues: quality and design of the product; marketing strategy; after-sales back-up; purchasing strategy; labour relations and how, and to what extent, to train the workforce. In a country which had a fairly 'closed' economy, with few imports and exports, it would not be too drastic for society if all companies and businesses were taking the wrong decisions: the very bad would go bankrupt and therefore be eliminated by the market mechanism, while the least bad would continue to survive, providing employment. In an economy as 'open' as Britain's is to imports and exports, however, it matters a great deal if companies take the wrong decisions because it is theoretically possible that they could *all* be eliminated by more efficient foreign businesses exporting into Britain. The more an economy is concentrated, where production of goods and services lies in the hands of relatively few industries and businesses, the more vulnerable it is to misjudgements by the managements of key companies. These premisses are the foundations upon which the arguments that are advanced in Williams *et al: Why are the British Bad at Manufacturing* are built.

The Williams *et al* study benefits from its eclectic approach and is strong on empirical data. The authors proceed by trying to analyse what it is that is peculiar to what they call the 'British national environment' which adversely conditions performance in business. They concentrate on four determinants, to which they attach the following labels: 'enterprise control over the labour process'; 'market structure and composition of demand'; 'the relation of manufacturing enterprise to financial institutions'; and 'the relation of manufacturing enterprise to government'.

The Williams *et al* study concentrates on reasons for poor *manufacturing* performance in Britain because they see it as a major determinant of the wider economic problems that afflicted the country in the post-war years. Obviously, manufacturing is only one part of the economy, and Williams *et al* see the problems that faced manufacturing as being different from the problems faced by other sectors.

For Williams and his colleagues, poor manufacturing performance is not the result, as some would claim, of one overriding condition, such as low investment or 'powerful' trade unions. For them the issue is much more complicated; different sectors of the economy have faced different situations and different problems. Nevertheless, they do seek to provide explanations which relate to Britain in national terms.

They start by noting certain characteristics of the British economy and the British manufacturing sector. They note that Britain has an 'open' economy and, as mentioned earlier, that the British manufacturing sector has become increasingly heavily committed to exports. They say:

> Through the first half of the 1960s, exports accounted for 17–18 per cent of UK manufacturers' sales, while by the end of the 1970s they accounted for around 30 per cent.[1]

This apparently good news, however, has to be set alongside the fact that Britain's export performance has, in relative terms, been poor in the post-war years.

> During the long boom of the 1950s and 1960s, Britain's share of world exports of manufactures declined propitiously; our share slumped from 19.8 per cent to 10.8 per cent in the fifteen years after 1955. This is the key indicator which shows the relative weakness of British manufacturing in the 1950s and 1960s when all the comparably sized industrial economies (like France, West Germany, Japan and Italy) maintained or gained trade share. It is gratifying to find that this slide was halted in the 1970s; after 1973, our share of world trade in manufactures seems to have stabilised at around 9 per cent.[2]

Williams *et al* produce evidence to show that foreign companies increased their share of the market for manufactures in Britain dramatically: between the mid-1950s and 1980 they increased their share from under 10 per cent to around 30 per cent.[3] Additionally, manufactures began to assume a greater proportion of the total import bill.

In the early 1950s, manufactures accounted for 20 per cent of our total imports, by 1970 they accounted for 50 per cent and by 1980 for almost 65 per cent.[4]

The thesis proceeds by recognising the importance of American-owned multinational corporations in Britain—accounting for a higher proportion of manufacturing production than in say, Germany or France—and the 'concentrated' nature of the British economy. To support this, they draw on figures which show that in 1949, the hundred largest manufacturing businesses in the United Kingdom produced 22 per cent of total manufacturing output; by 1970, this was 41 per cent.

The key point stemming from this is that the success or failure of the total manufacturing sector in the UK is dependent upon the activities of the top 100 or 200 companies. When they take decisions on marketing strategy, on product development and design, these decisions are crucial to the fate of the overall manufacturing sector. And, importantly, because many of the key companies are foreign-owned multinationals, many of the key decisions may be being taken in Tokyo or Detroit, where managements do not hold any particular allegiance to the British economy.

Seeking to find reasons for these economic problems, they first examine a series of issues under the heading 'enterprise control over the labour process'. Essentially, here, they are interested in looking at the incidence of strikes, 'bad' work practices and comparisons of productivity. In other words, are British workers more militant or lazy than their counterparts abroad?

First of all, they dismiss the argument that relatively poor manufacturing performance is due to strike-happy workers. Even in the period 1967–70, which was the high-point of industrial action, Britain was only around the middle of the advanced countries' strike league table in terms of days lost per 1,000 workers. As they acknowledge, the 'table' does not include unofficial stoppages, of which there were more in Britain than elsewhere, but they still contend that days lost due to strikes would not be a major determinant in poor manufacturing performance.

A second aspect examined in this area relates to productivity and labour costs. They point out that, by the mid-1970s, Britain had become a low-wage economy. In terms of productivity, Williams *et al* argue that while productivity *did* lag behind France and West Germany in the period 1955–60, it had caught up with them by 1969–70. Their conclusion is that:

The evidence shows that labour productivity performance is respectable in relative international terms.[5]

They argue that, even in sectors where productivity was undeniably low and strikes frequent, it was other factors which caused more problems. In car manufacturing, for example, where there were strikes and there was low productivity, they point to British manufacturers' failure to win export markets, which was caused by such things as poor product design and mistaken strategic decisions. Clearly, for Williams *et al*, the workers are not to blame.

A second heading they have designated for analysis is 'market structure and composition of demand'. The specific problem cited here is that British companies failed to adjust adequately to the composition of demand: manufacturers in Britain managed to produce products which met the home market but were unattractive to foreign consumers. As an example, they cite the British motorcycle industry. Here, the industry was ousted from its major market, the United States, because it failed to adjust to the new uses the machines were being put to: the new, booming 'Steve McQueen' leisure market, rather than low-cost, basic transport. Shipbuilding is also cited. British shipbuilders had concentrated their efforts into producing for British shipowners: but when the requirements of British shipowners changed, and they started buying big tankers and bulk carriers, British shipbuilders were unable to cope, having failed to adjust their production facilities to the new requirements. Shipowners therefore looked to South Korea and Japan, which could provide the goods, often from purpose-built greenfield sites. The forerunner of what is in 1989 called the Rover Group, the British Motor Corporation/British Leyland Motor Corporation, is also cited as an example. In the post-war era this company had failed to develop a distribution network in France and Germany, two of the biggest car markets in Europe. And obviously whatever the reason, the absence of such a network was a serious mistake. A key point that they make is that post-war governments in Britain have not taken these marketing problems seriously. Instead, governments simply channelled money into ailing industries, ignoring the marketing problems. Economists of the liberal school would argue, of course, that companies' marketing strategy is nothing to do with government; nor for that matter, should companies receive subsidies.

Williams *et al* move on to examine the relationship between financial institutions and manufacturing concerns in Britain. Within the ambit of that investigation, their findings can be summarised as follows:

(a) To a larger extent than elsewhere, British companies have financed their investment out of internally generated funds.

(b) The Stock Exchange, through the issuing of new shares, has, in Britain, been as important a provider of finance to firms as have the banks, which means that the Stock Exchange has been more important in Britain than in other advanced capitalist economies.

(c) The lending policy of the banks in Britain has been very conservative—they have considered it bad practice to lend long to companies whilst borrowing short from depositors.

(d) Contractual savings, such as those accumulated in pension funds and insurance policies, have been more important in Britain than elsewhere, and in the mid-1970s, accounted for between 35 and 40 per cent of household gross savings, as contrasted with 11–16 per cent in Germany and 3–4 per cent in France. Had these funds been channelled into industry, argue Williams *et al*, they could have provided an 'engine for growth'. But this did not happen for two reasons: pension funds and insurance companies have been buying shares in businesses from individuals rather than the corporate sector, so money has gone to individuals to finance consumption; and in order to safeguard the investments from a crash in any one sector, institutional investors spread the portfolio across a wide range of areas including property and government securities.

(e) The importance of the stock market in Britain, coupled with the very poor profit levels of the late 1960s, operated to create the environment within which a merger boom could take place. As companies could take over other companies on the basis of shares they issued themselves and by 'paper transactions', such mergers provided an easy route to growth for companies. The consequence of this merger boom was a greater concentration in the economy of Britain. In the end, this meant that a relatively small number of big companies were largely responsible for the poor manufacturing performance of the country as a whole. The corollary was that British companies discovered how to grow without having to make big profits. Another downside was that mergers created problems for management. The new, merged companies were often much more diversified in product range than they had been previously, and a lot of small plants, geographically fragmented, were put together under one owner. Obviously, this brought problems of organisation especially when the operations were not immediately rationalised, as Williams and his colleagues contend they were not.

Under a fourth section examining government economic policies, Williams *et al* offer a critique of those economists and political commentators who overemphasise the importance of macroeconomic policies, who hold that if only the right macroeconomic conditions could be maintained, then all else would be well, firms would respond to the conditions and prosper accordingly. According to the argument, the Keynesian economists and politicians of the 1950s and 1960s, who believed, above all else, in government manipulation of taxes, interest rate levels and the availability of credit to 'manage' overall demand in the economy, were guilty of this folly. In retrospect, although they were quite clearly wrong, they expected companies to perform in some way better under these 'managed' economic conditions.

The 'monetarists', who emphasised the need for governments to control the amount of money in circulation in the economy, are also criticised for apparently believing that all could be achieved simply by lowering inflation and eliminating all but the lowest-cost producers. Where competition is on a non-price basis, i.e. it is based on design, on after-sales service, on reliability, then eliminating all but the lowest price producers will not suffice. The phenomenal success of the German car manufacturer BMW in the 1980s was not the result of competing on price with other cars: it was due to a perception that the car was well engineered and well styled and the cultivation of an 'image' equated with success. And, after all, success breeds success.

To be fair to the Conservatives in government in Britain in the 1980s, 'monetarism' was only really fashionable with them at the beginning of the decade. Eventually, the term was dropped from their lexicon, the 'targets' for monetary growth were dropped and the Thatcher government settled into a much more traditional 'liberal political economy' stance: stressing the virtues of the free market, free trade, competition and private ownership. Moreover, they did, at least in their rhetoric, stress the need to improve the quality and design of British goods in the mid- and late 1980s.

Williams *et al* also dismiss a series of other macroeconomic policies which were widely believed to have been damaging to Britain's economy. On the 'stop-go' era of the 1950s and 1960s, when, because of balance of payments problems (i.e. people buying too many goods and services from abroad) economic growth was periodically cut off by governments and then restarted later, they point out that industries in other countries faced similarly severe fluctuations in demand but came through in better shape than their British counterparts. They cite cars in West Germany as an example. On the idea usually associated with the political right in Britain that company taxation has been too high, they point out that in the 1970s it was possible for many companies to adjust their affairs through 'creative accounting' so that they never paid any corporation tax at all; primarily as a consequence of generous depreciation allowances on equipment employed.

The Williams *et al* argument can be summarised as follows.

Manufacturing performance in Britain was poor for a number of different reasons concerned with the structure of the financial sector in Britain, problems of design and marketing, and the excessive faith of governments in macro-strategies such as Keynesianism or monetarism. Micro-problems, in other words, problems of individual industries, industrial sectors or companies, were largely ignored. Where they were attended to, by the Industrial Reorganisation Corporation of Harold Wilson's 1964–70 Labour government, for example, which encouraged mergers in the private sector in order to spur efficiency, or under the sectoral support schemes of the 1972 Industry Act (grants to industry for new product development payable providing certain criteria were fulfilled), such operations were either too short-lived or not properly developed.

The Williams *et al* thesis is not that governments should not intervene in the economy, but rather, that British governments have intervened either wrongly or not enough in certain areas. Managements are to blame for taking wrong decisions. The economy did not 'hang together' as a coherent whole, and the financial and industrial sectors had separate lives and separate directions.

NOTES

1. Williams *et al*, p. 10.
2. Williams *et al*, pp. 9–10.
3. Williams *et al*, p. 4.
4. Williams *et al*, p. 4.
5. Williams *et al*, p. 41.

11. The Trade Union 'Problem'

In the commentaries already presented, the trade union 'problem' in Britain has begun to rear its head as a chief culprit for the blame for poor industrial and economic performance. For many political commentators, it is trade unions that have, in the post-war era, been at the heart of Britain's economic problems.

In the centre parties in Britain—the Social and Liberal Democratic Party and the Social Democratic Party—for example, this view is supported. This was clear as they fought their election campaigns in 1983 and 1987: the SDP has favoured legislation to restrict union powers and the Liberal Party, forerunner of the Social and Liberal Democrats, has frequently argued for incomes policies, again designed to restrict the bargaining powers of unions in relation to wage levels. In 1989, it is not yet clear whether the Democrats, as most of the Social and Liberal Democratic Party prefer to be known, will continue this call, but the rationale for incomes policy, from a Keynesian perspective, is that the market for labour is perceived of as being inflexible downwards. In other words, when demand for labour falls off, or supply of it increases, as at times of unemployment, the price of labour, wages, does not fall. Trade unions do not allow them to fall. This can be inflationary as well as doing nothing to solve, indeed even producing, increases in unemployment. Incomes policy is supposed to dampen wage inflation while at the same time allowing increases in employment.

Trade unions are also a problem for what have been called here liberal political economists, which includes the leadership of the Conservative party, and therefore the Government of Britain, in the 1980s. For them, trade unions are a major obstacle to the workings of the market for labour: they prevent wages from falling when they otherwise would; they boost wages higher than they would otherwise be under 'market' conditions; they operate 'restrictive practices', entailing, for example, a far greater number of workers doing a particular job than is necessary; and, to boot, they have been undemocratic, not consulting their membership on important decisions, not regularly electing leaders, resulting in a 'zealotocracy' whereby a few, politically motivated zealots have ruled unions.

Liberal political economists accept the right existence of trade unions to exist—indeed, while their critics would suggest it was done for cynical, politically motivated reasons, liberal political economists were some of the most strident in arguing that Solidarity should be allowed to exist in Poland in the 1980s. But they argue that they should remain at the level of voluntary associations, offering services such as insurance, welfare provision, advice and representation with employers. Once they become coercive groups or private monopolies, forcing workers to join them and only allowing them to work for a company if specific rates of pay and conditions are met, then they become obstacles to the efficient working of the market for labour, and render the economy less efficient. It is in this light that trade unions have been viewed by liberal political economists in Britain in the post-war era.

Samuel Brittan, for example, an advocate of the free market, saw unions as being not only damaging to the national economy but also to workers themselves. He argued that they used the threat of strike action to force governments in the post-war era into a battery of unwise economic policies: price controls, subsidies to companies and consumers to keep down prices, high taxation, excessive government borrowing and excessive increases in the supply of money in the economy. They acted to prevent the movement of workers from declining sectors of the economy to expanding sectors by the 'distortions' to market rates of pay they produced; and thus they slowed economic growth. And, as some unions are stronger than others, it is the strong that can claim an unfair share of resources for their members: 'excessive' wage rates, government subsidies to the companies, subsidies to consumers by keeping the price down, or a tax on consumers where the price is kept higher than it would otherwise be in the case of a monopoly supplier. Other workers on the other hand are 'crowded' into fewer and lower-paid occupations. Moreover, the more militant a union, the more likely an employer is to replace workers by machine, becoming more capital-intensive, and in that sense it is argued that militant trade unionism causes unemployment.[1]

Enoch Powell, another economic liberal who rose to prominence as an influential and controversial figure in the Conservative party in the 1960s and 1970s, also saw trade unions as a problem, with the ability to stop markets from working effectively because of three 'special privileges' which they enjoyed. Powell listed them in the late 1960s as 'the freedom to intimidate'; 'the freedom to impose costs on others with impunity'; and 'the immunity of trade unions from actions of tort'.

Trade unions have their defenders, of course, especially on the left and centre-left of British politics. After all, they do have an important job to do in representing their members. And a worker who has been unfairly treated is more often than not completely powerless against an employer; indeed, a union itself can have its power significantly curtailed if it fails to represent a large proportion of the workforce. Unity is strength, as the old union maxim has it. Specifically, the so-called 'privileges' listed by Powell would, in left and centre-left eyes, represent no more than the right to pursue effective industrial action. The 1906 Trades Disputes Act, which overturned the famous House of Lords decision of 1901 which became known as the Taff Vale Judgement and which had allowed unions to be sued for civil damages, established many of these 'privileges'. Most of them remained intact even after the collapse of the TUC-inspired General Strike of 1926 and the miners were defeated the same year after a long and bitter struggle. Liberal political economists have seen it as being of key importance that these 'privileges' be removed so as to create a labour market that works as markets should—with flexibility, and price changes in line with the forces of supply and demand—and to bring about a much less militant, more compliant, workforce.

Liberal political economists usually absolve trade unions from direct responsibility for inflation. That is the responsibilty of governments who cause it by printing money, or borrowing excessively, or not actively promoting free markets. But they *are* blamed for many of the other ills that affect the economy. By preventing the market for labour operating effectively, and in particular by preventing competitive downward bidding for available jobs among the unemployed, they promote unemployment. Because of the restrictive practices they are said to operate, often insisting on higher manning levels and greater safety measures than might otherwise have been the case, they are accused of promoting low productivity and increasing firms' costs. Thus, in sum, liberal political economists see trade unions as helping to transform companies from co-operative ventures between managements and workers into arenas of conflict, playing out the class struggle at the expense of the economy. On many occasions they have been accused of attempting to usurp the 'management's right to manage': this accusation was levelled at the National Union of Mineworkers by the then National Coal Board and the Conservative government with an unusual ferocity during the 1984–5 strike against pit closures.

If trade unionism *per se* is seen as troublesome by many political commentators, then British trade unionism is seen as being particularly bad when compared with, say, the German variety. West Germany is often picked as the point of comparison because, for so long during the post-war period, Germany's industry seemed to flourish while Britain's seemed to lose ground.

While in Britain there has historically been a large number of unions competing against each other for members, different unions organising different workers with different skills, periodic outbursts of strikes not organised or sanctioned by the union leadership, in Germany, the picture could hardly be more different. Wolfgang Streek, writing in 1984, notes that the German system is a much more ordered system of collective representation:

> The number of unions in Germany is minute by British standards. Union members are organised regardless of their skill and occupation; craft unions making claims to job control or employment prerogatives do not exist; there are almost no unofficial strikes, and not many official ones either; collective bargaining is organised on an industry-wide basis and well-coordinated nationally; wage drift [wage inflation spreading from industry to industry] seems to be non-existent.[2]

If it is argued that post-war trade unionism has been strong in Britain, at least up until the 1980s, that has not always been the case. The nineteenth and, indeed, eighteenth centuries saw long struggles for the recognition of trade unions by employers and for their activities to become legal. Gradually, concessions were won with the 1906 Trades Disputes Act marking an important turning point.

The First World War saw shortages of civilian manpower, particularly of skilled workers. This led to inflationary pressure as the shortages exerted an upward pressure on wages. Strikes also remained a threat to the war effort. By the time of the Second World War, such risks could not be taken again, and the measures introduced to avoid them effectively ushered in a new, more co-operative relationship between the unions and the government. The defeat of France in May 1940 provided a new urgency and the Government took steps to put the country on a new footing. Changes were made to the personnel of the Government, the most important of which was the appointment of Ernest Bevin to the Cabinet, as Minister for Labour. Bevin had sat on the General Council of the TUC for twenty years. By 1940, he was the most influential trade unionist in the country. He was, effectively, the creator of Britain's largest trade union, the Transport and General Workers' Union. In the Cabinet his role was to ensure that labour always felt it possible to co-operate with the war effort, and also to act as labour's seat at the highest table of decision-making.

By the time of the 1945–51 Labour government, the first government after the war, trade unions appeared to be accepted fully as estates of the realm. Indeed, this was the phrase used by Harold Wilson, the then Labour prime minister in 1968, in a speech to celebrate the TUC's centenary:

> The TUC has arrived. It is an estate of the realm, as real, as potent, as essentially part of the fabric of our national life, as any of the historic estates.[3]

One of the key features in the post-war consensus was that, throughout their long period of government from 1951 to 1964, the Conservatives did not challenge this position of trade unions. This contrasted sharply with what was going on in some of the countries which were Britain's economic competitors. In the 1950s in Japan, for instance, public sector strikes were outlawed, and 'company unions' replaced more militant labour organisations after a series of lock-outs. The car manufacturer which in the 1980s calls itself Nissan, but at one time called itself Datsun, and which has enjoyed phenomenal post-war success, felt it necessary in 1953 to fight and eventually win against a militant shop-floor union which had organised a 100-day strike.[4]

It was in the mid- and late 1960s that trade unions in Britain really began to be singled out as a problem. Economic growth was the central aim of both the Labour and Conservative parties and it was being argued by many that the serious trade union 'problem' of the time, the 'wild-cat', unofficial strike, was inhibiting growth. It was the growth of shop-stewards' committees, providing an alternative focus of power to national trade union leaderships, which had occasioned most of these 'wild-cat' strikes: the 1960s saw a new wave of shop-floor militancy, especially in areas of high growth, such as car manufacture.

The first major response of Harold Wilson's Labour government was to set up the Donovan Commission in 1965 to investigate the problem. It reported in 1968, and argued that legislation on industrial relations should be avoided: 'voluntarism', as the basic characteristic of the British system, should be preserved. It did propose an industrial relations commission, although it was envisaged that this would have no powers to order or command: its powers would be limited to advice and clarification, and it would attempt to persuade parties to accept propositions.

The Labour government did, however, propose legislation. In a White Paper entitled *In Place of Strife*, the Government proposed to curb the 'excessive abuse' of trade union power. Barbara Castle, the Employment Secretary, supported by Harold Wilson, saw her major task as restoring the authority of national trade union leaders against the shop stewards. New powers would be given to the Employment Secretary to intervene, for example, in inter-union disputes to enforce solutions under the threat of fines. A new Commission on Industrial Relations would be set up to offer advice to the Employment Secretary, and the Government would have powers to enforce a 28-day conciliation pause to halt certan strikes, again under the possible sanction of fines.

The unions were outraged at what they saw as this threat to their autonomy. Marxists within the movement saw the proposals as a 'betrayal': the Labour government, they argued, had reneged on the working class and had become class collaborators with the ruling class enemy. But what these Marxists did not see, or did not want to see, was the urgent necessity for a system of industrial relations in Britain that helped, rather than hindered, industrial and economic progress. Whether the *In Place of Strife* proposals were the right system, of course, is another matter.

Opposition from the trade unions, then as in the late 1980s paymasters of the Labour party, was enough to defeat *In Place of Strife* before it could be turned into legislation. Opposition came from elsewhere as well—from Labour MPs, many of whom were sponsored by trade unions; but also from within the Cabinet itself, most notably perhaps from James Callaghan. It was he who, as Prime Minister, lost the 1979 general election, a defeat many attribute to the series of public sector strikes amongst council and health service workers, oil tanker drivers and others dubbed the 'winter of discontent'.

So instead of the creation of a legislative framework for industrial relations, a voluntary 'solemn and binding' agreement was struck between Harold Wilson and Vic Feather, the TUC General Secretary. It provided for sanctions such as the expulsion from the TUC of unions which refused to stop unofficial strikes.

The trade union 'problem', however, did not stop; and the next attempt at providing a legislative framework for industrial relations came with Ted Heath's Conservative government's Industrial Relations Act in 1971. Though the thinking behind this was largely similar to *In Place of Strife*, it was more ambitious. Amongst other provisions, the Act provided for a new National Industrial Relations Court with legislative backing, the registration of unions, sixty-day 'cooling off' periods in certain strikes, and a ban on the closed shop.

Again, the unions were furious. They saw the Act as nothing less than an attack on trade unionism itself. A wave of strikes resulted, the TUC adopted a policy of 'non-co-operation', and the political atmosphere, intensified by the militancy of miners who struck over pay in 1972 and 1974, was one of sour confrontation between trade unions and the Government. Early in 1972, the Government stopped using the Industrial Relations Act; the earlier imprisonment of dockers for contempt of court after falling foul of its provisions had been the point at which the Government judged it impolitic to press on.

When Labour returned to office in 1974, the industrial relations scene became more peaceful, at least for a time. It appeared for a while as if Labour was the only party which could 'work' with the trade unions. Its attitude towards them, as befits a party with such close links with them, was conciliatory. It introduced the Employment Protection Act in 1975 which increased workers' rights in terms of maternity leave, protection against discrimination against active trade unionists, lay-off pay at guaranteed levels, provisions against unfair dismissal. The Advisory, Conciliation and Arbitration Service (ACAS) was established as a government-funded body which would try to find solutions to disputes between workers and employers. The Health and Safety at Work Act was introduced in 1974 and provided for safety representatives on the shop floor. Many of these initiatives increased costs for employers.

The centre-piece of Labour's strategy for working with the trade unions was, however, the Social Contract. This was an agreement between the Labour government and the TUC. The trade unions agreed voluntarily to moderate their wage claims, while the Government, in turn, would ensure a higher 'social wage' i.e. welfare benefits would be increased, education and health services improved, and prices kept stable. For a while it worked, but 1978–9 saw an ignominious break-down with the 'winter of discontent' producing a wave of public and private sector strikes.

It was not until the Thatcher government era of the 1980s that a legislative framework was established for industrial relations in Britain. During the 1980s, the Government introduced four pieces of legislation which formed a key part of their overall economic and industrial policy programme. The first was the Employment Act 1980, introduced by Jim Prior when he was Secretary of State for Employment. This weakened picketing rights and rights to take secondary action; attempted to reduce the power of the closed shop; and weakened the recognition rights of unions. The Act made it illegal for employers to dismiss or otherwise discipline workers for not joining newly established closed shops unless a minimum of 80 per cent of those who would be affected by the closed shop had voted in favour of its introduction. The second piece of legislation was the Employment Act 1982. By this time Norman Tebbit had become Secretary of State for Employment. Tebbit was regarded as further to the right in political persuasion and harder on the unions. The Employment Act 1982 further weakened trade unions' abilities to organise and strike, and further weakened the closed shop; it also posed a threat to union funds. Fines of up to £250,000 could be levied on a union with over 100,000 members which disobeyed the law. The Act further clamped down on secondary action—strikes or other industrial action by unions not a party to the immediate dispute, or the picketing of places not directly involved in the dispute—by opening a wider range of activities to civil action. The third piece of legislation was the Trade Union Act 1984. This statute removed civil immunity from official strikes called without secret ballots; forced unions to ballot their members on the question of maintaining, or establishing, a political fund (a potential threat to the Labour Party which backfired, as all unions voted in favour of political funds); and asserted that all trade union leaders with voting rights on their union executive should be periodically elected by the membership.

1988 saw a further Employment Act, requiring all trade union leaders to stand for periodic election by secret postal ballot. Other provisions allowed union members to stop their leaders calling a strike without a secret ballot, and prevented unions from disciplining members who disobeyed a strike call, even where the strike was backed by a majority of the workforce.

Thus the policy stance of the Thatcher governments, adopting the classic liberal political economy position that trade unions are an impediment to economic and industrial progress, was to introduce two statutes which sought to regulate and restrict the power of trade unions, and a further two which attempted to shift the balance of power *within* trade unions as well as to further restrict their power to take industrial action. By ensuring that leaders were periodically elected, the Conservatives were hoping to provide for a move away from the situation in which, they argued, 'militant' trade union leaders were often leading an unwilling membership into disruptive industrial action. The view was that if the unions were 'given back to their members', then moderation would prevail.

Even these measures do not go far enough for some liberal political economists. There are those who would have strikes banned in certain 'essential' services, such as water supply, the fire service and electricity supply. The immediate difficulty there, of course, is in defining 'essential': if gas is 'essential', then why not coal?

Critics of the Thatcher government maintain that its industrial relations legislation is an undisguised attack on trade unionism. And, whether the Government was right or wrong, there is no doubt that they did see trade unions, or rather the way they behaved, as a major problem for the British economy, and they dealt with the problem accordingly.

Those on the left and centre left of British politics argued that very high unemployment had been deliberately created by the Thatcher government in order to smash trade unionism. Unemployment makes life difficult for unions in two ways: first, it reduces the membership of unions, and secondly it dissuades trade unionists, at least for a period, from pushing for 'excessive' wage increases because they fear the consequences—joining the dole queue. In 1979, 58.3 per cent of the workforce were members of trade unions. By 1985, this figure had fallen to 51.4 per cent. If the unemployed are considered to be potential workers, then in 1985, less than half of the potential workforce—44.7 per cent—were members of trade unions.[5] Others on the left argued that privatisation had been deployed as a means of curtailing union strength by breaking up some of the public sector unions: when the British Shipbuilders was a nationalised company, for instance, the trade unions could mobilise workers all across the country; when it was sold off to the private sector in individual yards, that potential ceased to exist.

In drawing conclusions on the trade unions and the 1980s Conservative governments, one factor has to be given prominence: the reduction in the number of strikes. 1988 saw the fewest number of days lost through strike action since 1935, down to a low in the year to June 1988 of 786 industrial stoppages.[6] What is not clear is why this should be the case. Is it the effects of higher unemployment, the trade union legislation, a mood of 'new realism' among the workforce, tougher managements? Perhaps it is a mixture of all of these.

The debate within the trade unions, and amongst prominent trade unionists, as to how to deal with the onslaughts from both the economy and the legislative programme has, by the end of the 1980s, effectively divided them into two camps. On the one hand, there are the 'new realists' epitomised by Eric Hammond of the EETPU and Bill Jordan of the AUEW. Their chosen stance has been one of co-operation with employers, a willingness to abide by no-strike agreements and to sign single-union deals with managements. Alongside this, they have sought to widen the range of services available to their members by becoming involved in the provision of training services, medical insurance, financial advice and so on. On the other hand, there have been those trade unionists who have argued that the 'new realist' response is really just a surrender to the capitalist class, and who have argued that conflict and struggle is the only way forward for trade unionists. These are epitomised by Arthur Scargill of the National Union of Mineworkers; Ken Gill, formerly of Tass and latterly of Tass's successor the MFS; and Ken Cameron of the Fire Brigades Union. As the only real political friends that trade unionists have are in the Labour party, and as trade unions are the paymasters of the Labour party, the political repercussions extend into the party itself. The outcome of the battle, if there is an outcome, may well help to determine what kind of party Labour will be in the 1990s.

Trade unions have their defenders as well as their detractors. On the left it is argued, for example, that the nature of trade union power is defensive and that, moreover, it should be viewed in relation to the power of capitalist companies. Trade unions, in this view, merely *react* to events: they do not set the agenda for investment decisions, marketing decisions, product design decisions. It is capitalist firms which can shift production to where they wish, can choose to increase or decrease production levels, can choose to update product design or leave things as they are. All these are management decisions, and if it is managements who have got them wrong, then it is they who should take the blame for poor industrial performance.

The TUC has offered this defence against the charge that unions are strike-happy:

> The country loses far more working days through ill health and accidents at work than it ever does through industrial action. In the period 1978/79, including the so-called 'winter of discontent', 25.5 million working days were lost because of disputes. At the same time 288 million days were lost through sickness.[7]

One's position on trade unions and trade union power largely depends on where one stands on the political spectrum. For liberal political economists, for the right in British politics, it is important that trade union power be drastically curtailed if not extinguished altogether. Others, not so far to the right, and often associated with what has been called the school of national political economy, suggest the creation of 'corporatist' structures as a way through: in other words the bringing together of the major interest groups from industry with government in a more or less formalised bargaining system. Ian Gilmour, for example, a minister in the first Thatcher government, and a prominent 'traditionalist' Tory of the old school, has argued for the establishment of

> a public, preferably televised, forum in which all the main interests can take part. . .the new body, which would only be advisory, has either to be an enlargement and extension of the

NEDC or a completely new institution. In it, the Government, the unions, industry including small businesses, and representatives of the consumer would all be brought together. . .Each one's claim to national resources can usually be granted in full only if another interest's claim is either rigorously scaled down or rejected altogether. The forum would make this truth clear; the present system obscures it by giving the impression that the struggles are merely between the Government and particular interests.[8]

On the left, and among those associated with what has been called the school of Marxist political economy, the way through involves nothing less than a transition to a new form of social and economic order involving public ownership of industry and business, and an extensive welfare state. And, indeed, immediately this is broached, it highlights a source of conflict within British social democracy and within the alliance of the trade unions and the Labour party. Unions and trade unionists see their primary task, rightly, to defend the pay, jobs and conditions of their members; for the most part it can be asserted that they have not developed any coherent vision of an alternative to capitalism. Socialists, of course, have, and it is this which can lead to conflict between trade unionists and their political allies if the latter have, for example, a plan for energy policy which involves the closure of nuclear power stations. Even if alternative employment is guaranteed at the sites of closure, the unions there would still resist the operation; the plan would still pose a threat to their power, existence and future.

NOTES

1. Brittan.
2. Streek.
3. Wilson, p. 533.
4. Glyn and Harrison, p. 50.
5. The *Financial Times*, 11 November 1987.
6. The *Guardian*, 19 August 1988.
7. *Hands Up for Democracy* (TUC Publications, 1983).
8. Gilmour (1983), pp. 208–9.

12. The Financial Sector

If trade unions are the *bête noire* of the right, then it has to be the City that has the equivalent role in left-wing demonology. The idea that it is the nature of the financial sector in Britain, the City and all that that conjures up, that is responsible for poor performance across the rest of the economy, is an all-pervasive one in the thinking of the left.

To refer to the financial sector as the City never was, and is increasingly less, accurate. Some of the largest financial institutions, such as the building societies, the Co-op Bank and insurance services and the TSB, have their roots far away from the Square Mile in London and other institutions have moved away from the Square Mile to secure larger and less expensive premises in which to house their dealing operations. So the financial sector, as defined here, covers a whole host of institutions: clearing banks, merchant banks, the Stock Exchange, Lloyd's, pension funds and insurance companies, building societies, unit and investment trusts and commodity markets.

It is argued by some people that there are certain differences between the financial sector in this country and that in comparable countries, and these differences have led to a poorer service to industry and therefore to poorer industrial performance. Most locate the first and central difference somewhere in antiquity. David Sainsbury, for example, notes that:

The fact that Britain was the first country to industrialize meant that there was no need to set up a system to channel funds on a continuous and large scale to industry. Businesses were able to start out small and grow by means of retained earnings.[1]

By contrast, in Germany and France there was a determined and conscious effort to catch up with Britain in industrialisation, and this led to the establishment of new financial institutions specifically for that purpose. He cites in particular the setting up of new banks in the 1850s in Germany. J.C. Carrington and G.T. Edwards make much the same point.

Non-provision of investment funds is however not the fault of the banking system; it is the consequence of an Anglo-Saxon economic history, in which the financial system and the industrial system have kept themselves quite distinct.[2]

Figures were given earlier which showed that a greater proportion of individuals' savings were tied up in insurance and pension funds in Britain than in, say, Germany or France, and this too is an important element to consider when examining the British financial sector. For what it means—or at least this is the argument—is that a huge amount of money for investment is in the hands of a relatively small number of insurance companies and pension funds. This presents certain problems for those who would see insurance companies and pension funds as a means of channelling finance to industry. First, while it is true to say that, through shareholdings, pension funds and insurance companies own large chunks of British industry, the number of companies that they are interested in investing in and providing finance for is severely limited. Pension funds and insurance companies require investments which need the minimum of management, and therefore often only 'blue-chip' (large and secure) companies qualify for their attentions. A whole range of companies fail to meet these requirements. Secondly, like any prudent investor, insurance companies and pension funds like to spread their risks: and so they will invest in property, government securities and, in the case of the railway workers' fund, even in art treasures, as well as in business. It is their duty, after all, to get the best possible return. Obviously, so the argument goes, a country which has more of its savings tied up in this fashion will be at a disadvantage in relation to comparable countries in terms of the provision of finance for industry and business. Indeed, in the 1980s Arthur Scargill and the NUM fought, and lost, a court battle against the then National Coal Board to try to prevent the mineworkers' pension fund from investing in competing industries such as oil, and in South Africa, for political reasons. And, as Richard Minns notes:

Since 1957, the value of personal wealth held in life assurance and pension funds has risen more rapidly than holdings of any other major type of financial asset, except for buiding society deposits.[3]

This channelling of a large proportion of personal savings into building societies is another distinctive feature of the British financial system. There has been some liberalisation in the late 1980s with regard to what building societies can do with their funds, enabling them to change their status from mutual institutions to joint stock companies so that they can raise money not just from small savers but also on the national and international money markets, to issue credit cards and personal loans, to own estate agencies and so on. But there are still restrictions, voluntary and involuntary, on what they can do with their money. They have not been, and are unlikely to become in the future, a source of finance for industry. Even the Abbey National Building Society, for example, which was the first building society to announce its intention in 1988 to change from mutual to public limited company status, has said in an information leaflet that on conversion:

Abbey National would be free to offer the same services [as a high street bank] but would retain its special character. Abbey National would be concentrating on providing personal financial services, rather than banking services for companies and the financing of overseas business loans.

Thus a large proportion of available funds in Britain is concentrated in the private house-owning sector. The political objective which lies behind this, and which has been a key priority of the Thatcher governments of the 1980s, may indeed be an honourable one: to raise the level of owner-occupation. But there are those who would argue that a cheap source of long-term finance for industry and business should be a greater priority.

These kinds of investment—mortgages for owner-occupied housing, life insurance and pensions—do, of course, receive favourable tax treatment in Britain, with tax relief on mortgages in particular resulting in the loss of millions of pounds of potential taxation revenue.

A major criticism of the British financial sector is that it is conservative by nature, unwilling to take risks, and has traditionally sought to lend only on a short-term basis to business while borrowing on a longer term. To do otherwise would be considered by the banking sector to be imprudent. David Sainsbury notes that banks in Britain have used more of a 'liquidation' approach to lending to business whereas German, French and Japanese banks have tended to favour more of a 'going concern' approach.

The 'liquidation' approach starts with the assets and liabilities of the company looking for funds, adjusts for what would happen in the event of a liquidation, and then aims to have a safety margin. The 'going concern' approach, on the other hand, makes the lending decision dependent on the ability of a company to serve the principal and interest on the loan.[4]

Particularly unfavourable comparisons are made between the British and German banking systems. In Germany, it is common for a company to have a sort of 'house bank' which acts as permanent financial adviser. There is rarely such close contact in Britain unless a company is preparing for a flotation on the Stock Market or is going into receivership. German banks also devote far more resources into researching industry and industrial problems, designating specialist staff for such purposes. Over-all, German banks are said to have a much closer relationship with industry and business.

If there are areas in British politics where there is potential for consensus, the City is not one of them. To the right and centre-right it is a series of highly successful financial institutions earning a valuable surplus on its trading abroad which as 'invisibles' contribute towards making sure the balance of payments does not drift too far into deficit. The left, on the contrary, sees the City as a drain on Britain's resources, syphoning off money overseas, wielding enormous political influence through its control over funds coming in and out of Britain and therefore the external value of sterling. Even the argument that investment managers for pension funds have a duty to provide the highest return is not immune from the onslaught. Richard Minns sums up their arguments well.

> There has been a huge increase in personal savings, over the last twenty years or so; this has been channelled into pension schemes and insurance policies of one sort or another; this has in turn resulted in a massive concentration of investment power in the City, through the merchant banks and insurance companies in particular. The huge savings mountain has been inserted into an internationally orientated financial system where returns on projects in the UK are assessed on a world-wide basis. The savings of future pensioners have been increasingly invested overseas and in short-term profits in the UK. This means that companies that employ future pensioners do not get funds for long-term productive investment in the UK. The jobs of future pensioners are thereby put at risk because of the approach to investment in the UK.[5]

The answer of the left is a familiar one: to provide more public sector control over the financial sector. In most cases this comes down to a proposal to nationalise banks, pension fund companies and insurance companies. The further left one travels, the more institutions are brought into the nationalisation net. The Labour party's policy in the mid and late 1980s was similar but more restricted: if elected to government it proposed to set up a National Investment Bank. This would be publicly owned and the intention would be for it to provide long-term loans below the market rate of interest to industry and business and, in particular, to high-tech sectors.

To the right and centre-right, of course, all this is nonsense. The National Investment Bank would simply involve civil servants or some other bureaucrats in trying to spot projects that would work, and why should they be any better at it than businessmen and bankers working under commercial pressures? Introducing a nationalised sector into the financial arena would simply introduce what they see as having been wrong with all the other previously nationalised areas—overmanning, delays in decision-making, political interference by governments—into what is a very successful part of the economy.

It is impossible to state with any certainty whether or not the financial system in Britain has hampered industrial development. The two sectors themselves, industry and finance, are so vast and varied that they are not easily delineated. The City itself defends its position by saying that if there have ever been shortages, they have been shortages of good projects from industry rather than shortages of finance from the City. A study published in the *Oxford Review of Economic Policy* in 1987, and entitled 'Corporate Finance and Investment' did, however, conclude that industry had not been served as well in Britain as its counterparts in West Germany, and more especially Japan. The study found that Japanese banks would provide a far larger amount of industry's investment needs, lend for longer periods and at favourable interest rates where a company is facing difficulties.[6]

Concerned at the abiding speculation that there was something in the relationship between the financial sector and industry that was problematic for the latter, the CBI set up a task force to investigate, the findings of which were published in October 1987.[7] Broadly speaking, the City was found not guilty of serious shortcomings in dealing with industrial customers. Among its conclusions were that a general shortage of finance for good small or high-risk projects was not apparent, though such finance might be expensive; that the majority of financial institutions *are* long-term investors; and that the inadequate profitability of companies has been more of a pressure against long-term investment than short-term considerations in the City. The report concluded by calling for greater institutional links between industry and the City, acknowledging that communications between the two sectors were far better in West Germany, France and Japan. This report itself, however, was open to the criticism that it did not fully explore the role of the banks, really the key institutions in terms of lending to industry. Moreover, it seemed to skirt over the *demand* side of the problem of short-termism in lending: even if practices have changed recently, companies turned down when asking for long-term loans will not be rushing to ask for them again.

NOTES

1. Sainsbury, p. 8.
2. Carrington and Edwards, p. 219.
3. Minns, p. 11.
4. Sainsbury, p. 10.
5. Minns, pp. 37–8.
6. *Oxford Review of Economic Policy*.
7. Confederation of British Industry/City Task Force.

Conclusion

It is unlikely that any of the explanations for Britain's relatively poor industrial performance outlined here are sufficient, by themselves, to account for that performance. All are open to various criticisms and, if there is an 'explanation', it is more likely to comprise a collection of theories, only some of which have been considered here.

It is likely, for example, that Empire had a mixed legacy for British industrial performance. True enough, it did provide, for a long period, cheap raw materials for British companies and more or less captive markets for their products. But these captive markets may also have had a harmful effect on British industry: firms may have seen little need to innovate, update their products, ensure their quality was up to scratch. Once the captive markets became open as the British colonies achieved their independence over the post-war years, British companies might have been unprepared for the stiff competition they found from companies which *had* had to innovate and ensure quality to survive.

More specifically, Wiener's thesis of the absence of a real 'industrial bourgeoisie' and the hegemony of the 'English countryside culture' seems over-impressionistic. Does one really have to belong to a particular class in order to do something? It helps, of course: if one's father is a successful businessman then it is likely that one will be given a head start in knowing how to run a business. But if the motivation is money-making, and surely it is, then were not the maligned aristocratic class pretty good at that anyway? And on the cultural front, can one not appreciate Wordsworth, can one not aspire to live in a large country house, and yet at the same time be industrious?

While the case put forward by Williams *et al* has its merits, it falters by seemingly absolving the workers from any blame whatsoever. When one looks back at the 1960s and 1970s—two crippling official miners' strikes in 1972 and 1974 and an unofficial one in 1969, dozens of 'wild-cat' strikes in the car industry in the 1960s, work-ins at Upper Clyde Shipbuilders in the early 1970s, strikes by lorry drivers, railway operators, dockers, construction workers, firemen in 1977, the 'winter of discontent' in 1978–9—can such an assertion really be substantiated? Figures might be produced which show that Britain's strike record was not so bad compared with other countries, or that more days were lost through illness, but the unquantifiable aspect is that employers and managers may have felt constrained in their behaviour, may have shrunk from taking decisions which may have improved business, for fear of what the unions *might* do. I remember an example from my own time in industry. I worked, for part of the 1970s, for a subsidiary of the British Steel Corporation. This company manufactured road springs for British vehicle manufacturers. At the time, all the steel that was used in this manufacturing process came from the British Steel Corporation itself. The management of the subsidiary then took a decision to obtain some Japanese steel to test its price and quality. It had to be smuggled onto the shop floor and tested in secret, for fear of how the unions might react. It may well be, of course, that unions had legitimate grievances in the 1960s and 1970s—that is a debate outside the scope of this essay. But what cannot be denied is that industrial relations were 'troublesome' during the period, and that can only have damaged industrial performance.

When one turns to the financial sector, although there may indeed be grounds for criticism of its relationship with industry, one cannot help but be struck by the idea that here is a tailor-made scapegoat for the left. Here was everything the left loved to hate: the old school tie; people dealing in commodities that would never be delivered to anyone; the idea that the value of a company, through its share price, could vary enormously in one day, when the left were certain that what really made a company was the hard-working nature of its underpaid, blue-collar workforce; the later expensive 'Yuppiedom' of Porsches and car-phones and expensive Wharfside flats. And, of course, the City obliged by playing out the characterised stereotype to the full. Even if it could be proved, categorically, that there was nothing at all wrong with the way the financial sector operated, nothing at all wrong in the relationship between it and industry, any self-respecting left-winger would have to find something wrong with this body of people and institutions. That is not to argue that there is nothing wrong with the financial sector in Britain: there possibly is. But in politics, people adopt positions of such entrenchment that their vision and their objectivity is blurred by pre-conceived perceptions.

PART THREE
Issues and Problems

13. Department for Enterprise and Regional Policy

January 1988 marked an important juncture in the progress of government policies towards industry in Britain, seeing the publication of Lord Young's White Paper *DTI—the department for Enterprise*. By the late 1980s, Lord Young had become one of the most influential ministers in Mrs Thatcher's government, close to the Prime Minister herself, and having held the cabinet positions of Minister without Portfolio, Secretary of State for Employment and, latterly, Secretary of State for Trade and Industry.

The launching of the White Paper marked an attempt to find a new role for the Department of Trade and Industry, which Lord Young wished henceforth to be known as the Department for Enterprise. Under previous governments, pursuing a policy of maintaining a nationalised industry element within the economy, and/or a policy of selective government intervention in industry, there had been a clear and obvious role for a Department of Industry or a Department of Trade and Industry. That role was to monitor most of the nationalised industries, and where there was a policy of selective intervention, to provide and monitor that intervention. Under a social market regime, however, in which government attempts to disengage itself from direct involvement with industry, its role is less clear. Indeed, once it has divested itself of its nationalised industry responsibilities, there would be very little for it to do, except, perhaps, to enforce anti-monopoly policy.

The central themes of the White Paper were to stress that the Government would continue to attempt to foster the 'enterprise culture'. Through deregulation of industries, privatisation and encouragement of competition, it would seek to open up and promote free markets. It would seek to encourage closer links between industry and education; the objective would be to give two or more weeks of work experience to school pupils before they left school, and to enable ten per cent of school teachers every year to gain personal experience of the world of business and industry. In keeping with the liberal political economy stance, the Department for Enterprise would seek to disengage itself from decision-making as regards industry and business. Decisions would be taken by sovereign individuals in the market place.

> The central theme of our policies remains the belief that sensible economic decisions are best taken by those competing in the market place. The responsibility of Government is to create the right climate so that markets work better and to encourage enterprise. The aim of our policy is thus to encourage the process of wealth creation by stimulating individual initiative and enterprise and by promoting an understanding of market opportunities combined with the ability to exploit them.[1]

If high taxation, an anti-enterprise culture within society and misguided government intervention in the industrial economy had been prime candidates in the downfall of Britain's economy, as the White Paper suggests, then so had red tape and the dead hand of state bureaucracy on business. Thus, the White Paper promised to 'remove the burden of unnecessary Government regulations from business and to improve regulation where it is absolutely essential'.

For this purpose, the Enterprise and Deregulation Unit (EDU), established by Lord Young, was carried over from the Department of Employment to the Department of Trade and Industry, and would continue its work of cutting back on red tape across the whole of government.

The White Paper also launched changes in regional policy, the oldest form of what used to be called 'industrial policy'. Regional policy started in 1934, with the passing of the Special Areas Act; originally, it was the north-east of England that benefited from advance factory building by the forerunner of the state-owned English Estates Corporation. Regional policy, essentially, means the provision of money or other inducements by governments to companies which are prepared to locate or expand existing operations in areas of the country regarded to be relatively impoverished.

In fact, during the 1980s, regional disparities in prosperity looked like becoming a major political issue. Often somewhat misguidedly called the 'north–south' divide, critics of the way the economy was being managed pointed to higher rates of unemployment, lower levels of prosperity, and greater intensifications of urban deprivation affecting northern towns and cities when compared with their southern counterparts. The mid- and late 1980s economic revival, they said, was a patchy one which was leaving economic wastelands in Scotland, parts of South Wales, the north of England and the West Midlands. This 'divide' was mirrored politically with Labour being the strongest party in all the major northern cities, like Liverpool, Manchester, Leeds, Newcastle and Glasgow, while the Conservatives were in a seemingly impregnable position in the relatively prosperous south. From Labour's point of view, this in itself was a disturbing factor. It was beginning to appear as if Labour was only popular with the dispossessed and the relatively underprivileged; while the Conservatives were perceived by many to be associated with the prosperous, affluent and successful. The irony of this, of course, is that it was arguably the policies of the Conservatives which provided for relative deprivation in certain areas with the slimming down of so many industries such as coal, steel, shipbuilding and car manufacture. That is not to say that such policies were not necessary: that is a different debate.

As a broad-brush picture those who argued that there was a north–south divide in the 1980s were largely correct. It would be wrong, however, to assume that deprivation did not exist in the south and prosperity did not exist in the north. Parts of Cornwall suffered fairly heavy unemployment, and some of the London boroughs such as Hackney and Haringey suffered extremely severe deprivation. In the north, property prices in parts of south Manchester and large parts of Cheshire were akin to those found in Surrey; and the prosperity of places such as Harrogate, Beverley, Wetherby and the south-western flanks of Sheffield such as Dore belied attempts to categorise the north as poor and the south as rich.

The rationale behind regional policy is, nevertheless, clear: the aim is to enhance the prosperity of the poorer regions and presumably, at the same time, preserve the social stability of the more prosperous southern regions by removing the temptation for hundreds of thousands of northerners to descend upon them looking for jobs.

The White Paper announced that as from April 1988, the 'automatic' assistance that had previously been provided to any firm of any size locating or expanding in development areas (the least prosperous regions) would be ended: finance from government might still be available, but it would be on a more selective basis. Regional aid had, in any case, been diminishing for some time: It had been £888 million in 1982–3, but provision for 1988–9, including both automatic and selective regional aid, stood at £545 million. From April 1988, a company requesting selective regional aid would have to prove that, without the aid, the investment would not take place. The *Financial Times*, in a leader of 13 January 1988, thought this policy shift unwise:

> The proposals for regional policy look especially ill-judged. The Government has steadily reduced support for the regions since 1979. Lord Young is going further even than Mr Norman Tebbit in 1983 and abolishing regional development grants, which provide automatic assistance for companies if they invest in depressed areas. In future, companies will get money only at the discretion of civil servants. What are needed are non-discretionary incentives focused on labour rather than capital. The shift towards discretion. . .is likely to dissuade some companies from even considering a move out of the prosperous south-east.

Criticisms of the change took two forms. One, epitomised by the above comment, saw it as a return to the 'Whitehall knows best' syndrome. Within the Conservative party, the most prominent critic in this vein was Norman Tebbit, himself a former Secretary of State for Trade and Industry, and former Chairman of the party, who argued that there was a danger of civil servants becoming 'unduly embroiled in taking commercial decisions on behalf of the companies'.[2]

The other criticism turned on the argument that this policy change was further evidence that the Thatcher government did not care about the regions, saw no political advantage in caring about them (for many of the constituencies within them were solid Labour), and was therefore prepared to see ever-widening disparities in prosperity in different parts of the country. Leon Brittan, another former Trade and Industry Secretary in the Thatcher government warned just after the publication of the White Paper that an 'active and vigorous regional policy must remain the top priority of government'.[3]

The cost of the jobs created under regional policies in the past has undoubtedly been high. It was revealed in 1979, for example, that the cost to the taxpayer of each of the 450 permanent jobs created by an inward investment into Ayrshire by the Swiss multinational Hoffman La Roche, amounted to £100,000. The company received further government aid in 1980 to build a railway siding, pushing the cost per job still higher. Another multinational, this time the American company Dow Corning, received £34 million in regional aid assistance from the first Thatcher government in 1980 for investment in South Wales. This meant that the estimated 125 permanent jobs created by the company cost the taxpayer £272,000 each.

Not all projects were as expensive as these, but there is a good deal of evidence to support the contention that regional aid has been an expensive way of creating jobs. Figures of anything between £30,000 and £60,000 are often quoted as the cost per job under regional assistance in the late 1970s and the 1980s. Moreover, there have been a number of spectacular failures of firms lured to the regions by regional aid. The Linwood car plant, for example, opened in 1963 in Scotland. Originally owned by the Rootes Group, who were later taken over by Chrysler and then later by Peugeot-Citroën, it closed ignominiously in 1981.

Linwood represented a classic case of regional policy failure. Pressurised to head northwards by a Conservative government which refused industrial development certificates (in other words, planning permission) for the establishment of a site at Coventry at the heart of the motor industry, Rootes ended up in Scotland. At the time, car manufacturing was expanding rapidly in Britain. The setting-up of this plant in Scotland was expected by the government of the day to engender other development in the locality, perhaps in component manufacture. But the problems of being 250 miles away from the main production centres in Coventry, which meant that components had to be hauled across the country, together with the distance from the major markets of the south-east, were never overcome.

Another car plant owned originally by the Triumph Motor Company (the remnants of which formed part of what became known as Rover Group in the late 1980s), at Speke near Liverpool, which was set up in 1959 after government pressure, closed in 1978. Again the plant had faced the problems of hauling components across the country, and the distance from major markets. Tractor production at Bathgate in Scotland, again run by a forerunner of the Rover Group lured there by government persuasion, also failed to survive.

In Northern Ireland, two other projects aimed at increasing employment in the province lost large sums of taxpayers' money: the DeLorean car manufacturing operation, which opened in 1979 and closed in December 1982, taking with it £78 million of public funds; and the Lear Fan experimental aircraft operation, which the Government decided to back in February 1980 and which was eventually wound up in 1985, losing £56 million in government assistance. Both projects called into question the competence of government ministers and civil servants in their dealings with businessmen. Parliament's Public Accounts Committee, which monitors the spending of public money, reported in 1986 that the loss on the Lear Fan project could and should have been avoided.[4] An adequate financial appraisal had not take place. The same committee commented in 1984 on the DeLorean project:

> We can only conclude, therefore, that the prospect of creating large-scale employment in West Belfast proved so irresistible to DOC [Northern Ireland's Department of Commerce] as to diminish its sensitivity to the commercial risks involved, impair its judgement and lead to the wrong decisions being taken.[5]

The report noted that no attempt had been made to investigate the creditworthiness of Mr DeLorean himself, an American citizen, and that British government representatives

> made no attempts to obtain reports into the projects from any banks or financial institutions in the USA. This must be regarded as a grave omission.

There have, of course, been some successes in regional policy. Ford's car plant at Halewood, and General Motors' plant at Ellesmere Port, both on Merseyside, have survived. But the overall picture is not a happy one. A large question mark has hung over British Steel's Ravenscraig plant, which was located there after political arm-twisting by Harold Macmillan's Conservative government, for some time.

The effectiveness of regional incentives as a draw to private investors must also be in question. Businessmen and women, if they are to be successful, have to be concerned about the practicalities of operating a business. Are the communications and transport facilities good? Are the markets nearby? Are there skilled people in the locality to operate the design, marketing, quality control or other vital functions? If not, would they be prepared to move to this area? What about the rest of the labour force in the area? Does it have a reputation for militancy? The lure of government money to locate in a particular area will often be insufficient if the other factors are wrong. Merseyside's reputation for trade union militancy, together with its extensive urban deprivation and generally run-down condition, have done little to attract investors.

On the other hand, if governments were to wash their hands of regional assistance completely, then disparities in wealth between different parts of the country would presumably be exacerbated. Free marketeers, of course, would deny this. Under their conception of reality, people from depressed areas would have to move to find jobs, or, alternatively, offer to work for wages lower than firms elsewhere have to pay. In that way, private business would take rational decisions to locate in the depressed regions. In reality, however, the south-east, with all its natural advantages as the centre of government, the centre of the corporate and financial world, the biggest market in the country, the closest to Europe, would continue to prosper. But it might also 'overheat', becoming more heavily populated and congested, facing ever more escalating property prices and generally becoming a more unpleasant place to live in. This would provide another argument in favour of regional aid.

Regional assistance also provided the bulk of taxpayer assistance to inwardly investing multinationals; its diminution might damage the prospects of such firms locating in Britain, especially when other countries continue to allocate it automatically. The Chief Executive of Inward, the agency responsible for attracting investment into the north-west of England, for example, was quoted in the *Financial Times* of 13 January 1988, as saying:

> Removal of the absolute certainty that grants will be available will not be helpful to the promotion of the UK overseas.

Dr John Bridge, Chief Executive of the Northern Development Company, responsible for attracting investment to the north-east and Cumbria, concurred.

> It is vital that the new discretionary system is applied as generously as the old, otherwise we will lose international competitiveness.[6]

The Department of Trade and Industry, after the 1988 White Paper, bagan to refer to its policies as enterprise initiatives. One of the major enterprise initiatives launched after the White Paper was government sponsorship of the use of design, marketing, quality management and manufacturing systems consultants by small and medium-sized businesses. Businesses with under 500 employees could tap a fund of £50 million provided for this purpose for 1988–9, initially supporting 1,000 consultancy projects a month. Half of the cost of the consultancy project would be met by the company; the other half by the Government. In the depressed regions, the Government would fund two-thirds of the cost.

This enterprise initiative was certainly a boon for private sector consultants; and it reflected the Government's justifiable concern that British companies were losing out to foreign competitors on non-price factors such as poor design or quality. But it sits uneasily with the rhetoric of a free-market government, which elsewhere is quite prepared simply to let private corporate management take decisions in the knowledge that they will be the right ones. This enterprise initiative is, in a new way, another form of government intervention.

The White Paper also announced the end of most grants to individual firms for high-tech projects, though a few exceptions would be made and high-tech research was to continue under the European Community's 'Esprit' project. Policies to promote competition within the economy were to be strengthened, and inquiries by the Monopolies and Mergers Commission as to whether mergers of firms are in or against the public interest were to be speeded up.

It will be some time before a judgement can be made as to whether the Department for Enterprise, and the enterprise initiatives can be judged a success. Indeed, before any judgement can be made, criteria would have to be laid down as to what 'success' constitutes. What would have happened in the absence of the enterprise initiatives? There was a time, in the 1950s, 1960s and 1970s, when people would have argued that a minister coming new to a department, as Lord Young did to Trade and Industry, would try to 'empire build', seeking to expand the department's powers and therefore his own role. That accusation could not be levelled against Lord Young, who, quite clearly, fervently believes in *less* government, *less* bureaucracy, *less* 'meddling'. One must accept, therefore, that the 1988 White Paper represents a genuine attempt to find a new role, and forge a new direction, for the Department of Trade and Industry in its new circumstances. The sceptics, however, remained. Samuel Brittan, an advocate of free markets and privatisation, and often therefore a friend of the Thatcher government's economic policies, felt justified in commenting in the *Financial Times* of 18 January 1988:

> What then are the reservations? By no means the least important objection is to the particular hype in which the White Paper is written. . .The 'people who make it happen' are 'championed' several times. Policies have been replaced by 'initiatives', usually with enterprise added. Many parts read like a send-up of Thatcherism by a hostile satirist.

NOTES

1. Department of Trade and Industry, Cmnd 278.
2. The *Guardian*, 13 January 1988.
3. The *Guardian*, 13 January 1988.
4. The *Times*, 11 July 1986.
5. House of Commons 25th Report from Committee of Public Accounts 1983–4.
6. The *Financial Times*, 13 January 1988.

14. Nationalisation and the Public Ownership of Industry

The public ownership of industry, in a variety of forms, came to Britain in three phases. The first was in the early part of the twentieth century. It was characterised by a gradual accretion of publicly owned enterprises rather than a concerted centralised effort to develop them. In this period, some municipalities began to operate gas and electricity supply systems, often alongside privately owned companies supplying the same services. Another publicly owned trading institution, the Post Office, was set up in 1919 as a government department. And an important prelude to the nationalisations instigated by the Labour government after the Second World War was the establishment of the Central Electricity Board (CEB) in 1927 by Stanley Baldwin's Conservative government. The electricity industry, with good reason, was regarded as being strategic; industrial development throughout the land would be dependent upon a national transmission network which the CEB would construct and operate. The CEB's other function was to control, but not own, the major generating stations. Other pre-war public enterprises, to use an all-embracing term, were the BBC, Imperial Airways and the London Passenger Transport Board.

The next, and major, phase of public ownership followed the election of the first majority Labour government immediately after the Second World War in 1945. Over the lifetime of this government, 1945–51, a host of industries were brought into public ownership. In terms of the labour force, the size of the public sector was increased by about two million employees. The nationalisation programme involved a major transfer of power over the economy from disparate private companies to the public sector. The coal industry was nationalised, and the British Transport Commission, established to take into public ownership and oversee transport provision had, by 1948, organised the nationalisation of the railways, the canals, the majority of the docks, many bus operations and most of the road haulage industry which was operating for hire. Iron and steel were nationalised. The gas and electricity industries were brought into full public ownership. Essentially, the industrial infrastructure of Britain—energy, transport and communications—was brought under state control.

The use of the term 'nationalisation' to indicate public ownership became common, with the new publicly owned industries being referred to as 'nationalised industries'. The use of this particular terminology was meant to implant the idea that what was being done was 'in the national interest', and that the industries were owned by the 'nation'.

These nationalisations took place as part of Labour's commitment to the controversial Clause IV, Part IV, of its constitution, which calls for the public ownership of the means of production, distribution and exchange, but also as a central part of the economic reconstruction programme that everybody agreed was necessary after the Second World War. Even the forces of the right largely acquiesced in the nationalisations: whole sections of British industry were suffering from underinvestment as resources had been devoted to the war effort. Winston Churchill, for example, accepted the principle of the nationalisation of the coal industry.

There were, however, tensions within the Labour party and the Labour government as to how far the nationalisation programme should go. Then, as in the late 1980s, the Labour party was a broad coalition of social democrats and socialists; centre-left and left in varying intensity. There were those on the left of the party who wanted public ownership to go much further: into shipbuilding, motor vehicle production, pharmaceuticals and a whole range of other industries. There were others, centred around Herbert Morrison, who thought they should consolidate the moves they had already made. Morrison, Deputy Prime Minister in Attlee's government, thought that to go further would alienate the electorate. It was these 'consolidationists' who were to triumph in Labour's electoral programmes in the 1950s and in their governmental policy in the 1960s.

So the Labour governments of 1964–70 renationalised the steel industry in 1967, and reorganised some existing nationalised industries, setting up the Girobank within the Post Office, but otherwise left well alone. It was not until the 1970s that a third phase of nationalisation was to emerge and that was largely influenced by crisis management. It was Mr Heath's Conservative government which nationalised the aerospace division of Rolls-Royce in 1971, for example, to stave off bankruptcy, while Labour took British Leyland (renamed various times, its descendant is known as the Rover Group) into public ownership in 1975 in order to stop that company going down. The Labour government of 1974–9 also nationalised the shipbuilding and aerospace industries, although there had been considerable state involvement in both industries prior to this, particularly in relation to defence contracts. Massive financial assistance for the shipbuilding industry had been provided by the Government anyway, prior to nationalisation, indicating the weakness of the industry. Labour also carried out one 'strategic' public enterprise operation: the creation of the British National Oil Corporation (BNOC). BNOC had the right to buy 51 per cent of oil from North Sea producers, as well as the right to explore for, and extract, oil. By this mechanism, the Government hoped to exert a large measure of control over the price of North Sea oil, and the rate of development and exploitation within the industry. Additionally, BNOC would yield information on operating costs and availability of resources invaluable to a government wrestling with the problem of deciding how much to tax American multinationals investing in and developing the oilfields without scaring them away.

The public corporation, based on the BBC structure, was the chosen form of organisation for the nationalised industries. The idea behind this was that a body of capable people would be appointed to the top management of a corporation and would be more or less autonomous from the Government, able to manage as they saw fit. The idea, again associated with Herbert Morrison, was that the Government would keep an 'arms-length' relationship with the industries: avoiding interference unless it was deemed absolutely necessary. It was hoped that by minimising political interference, management of the highest calibre would be attracted to these mammoth centralised undertakings.

But the public corporation, as an instrument of industrial policy, had its limitations. Taking the whole of an industry into public ownership was not the most flexible of economic tools, and not suitable for many smaller, but highly important, industrial sectors such as the high-tech industry. So a further innovation of the 1974–9 Wilson-Callaghan Labour government was the establishment of state holding companies. Under the 1975 Industry Act the National Enterprise Board (NEB) was created, alongside its much smaller 'sister' agencies, the Scottish Development Agency

(SDA) and the Welsh Development Agency (WDA).

The chief task of the NEB was to extend the state's involvement in the economy into the developing and profitable high-tech sectors of the industrial economy. The mechanism by which this would happen would be via an equity shareholding by the NEB in the developing sectors. In this way, companies would receive finance from government without incurring a huge debt and, from the government's point of view, it would be an investment which would repay itself in years to come. As well as the promotion of high-tech industry, the NEB had other roles: to contribute towards the revitalisation of the regions (with the SDA responsible for Scotland and the WDA for Wales); to promote small businesses; and to supervise nationalised companies allocated to it.

The powers of the NEB, however, were far more restricted than the left of the party would have liked. For a start, it was only able to buy shares from shareholders who wished to sell them. Secondly, it was usually required to charge commercial rates of interest on money it lent and to look to profitability from investments. Thirdly, the key, full-time members of the board of the NEB appointed by the Labour government were drawn from the ranks of private business. Although the board contained four trade unionists as part-time members, it was unlikely that the full-time members—Lord Ryder, who had spent time with Reed International, and was Chairman to July 1977, Sir Leslie Murphy, his successor as Chairman, who had worked in the petroleum industry and in merchant banking and Richard Morris from Courtaulds, who was Sir Leslie's replacement as Deputy Chairman —all of whom were drawn from the private sector, would be attractive to Labour's left. They appeared to have little in common with the socialist aspirations of the Labour movement. Michael Edwardes (now Sir Michael), for example, who had spent much of his business career with the Chloride Group, was another part-time member of the NEB. And yet, as he made clear in his book of reflections on his time at the then BL car company from 1977 to 1982, his philosophy appeared to be the very antithesis of what the NEB and Labour's industrial strategy stood for.

> Politics and business don't mix. . .Politics, with its focus on the day-to-day events which catch the headlines, cannot cope with the ups and downs of a company like BL, generating pressures to intervene to which ministers cannot and should not bow. Both politicians and businessmen find involvement with each other time-consuming and distracting from their more central tasks. They are generally not on the same wavelength.[1]

Thirdly, the finances available to the NEB were far less than the left of the Party had hoped; it was given an initial statutory borrowing limit, later extended, of £1,000 million. Additionally, instead of pursuing the role that had been envisaged for it—a dynamic, thrusting, 'entrepreneurial' arm of the state pulling along behind it a private sector reluctant to see profits accruing to the public exchequer—the NEB got saddled with two of the biggest loss-makers in the public domain: BL and Rolls-Royce Aerospace. Up to March 1979, these two companies took 90 per cent of the NEB's financial resources.

Part of the theory behind the NEB was that it would be able to provide finance for high-technology projects where it would otherwise not be forthcoming from traditional financial institutions which the left argued were only interested in short-term profits and would lend only conservatively.

This body was not the vehicle of socialist reconstruction that had been envisaged by the left of the Labour party. In retrospect, and reflecting the ideological conflicts within the party, the left now condemn it in the form in which it was implemented as being one more vain attempt by a Labour government to 'manage capitalism better than the Tories can'; in effect, an appeasement of capitalism rather than a challenge to it.

The Industrial Reorganisation Corporation of the 1960s was similarly condemned. Essentially, and paradoxically, the most severe criticisms of the NEB and Britain's nationalisation programme come from an unholy alliance of the left and right: those from the Marxist school of political economy and those from the liberal school. To the former, there was not enough nationalisation, the previous private owners of industry received too much compensation, and nationalised companies were run to supply, on a cheap basis, capitalism's industrial infrastructure. To the latter, public 'confiscation' of private property is simply wrong, and public ownership inherently inferior to private, in terms of efficiency. The true friends of nationalisation as it occurred in Britain could only be found in the national school of political economy, and even there, as the years passed, their numbers dwindled.

This is the nub of the problem of trying to analyse the aims and performance of publicly owned industry: different people wanted different things from it, and what they wanted, they wanted to differing extents. Thus a variety of motives for public ownership, of industry and other economic sectors, in one form or another can be identified.

The first is ideological. While for liberal political economists, and the right in British politics, the right to own wealth and property is sacrosanct; for the Marxist left, British society is class-based. There is a class which owns the wealth—the industry, the land, the property—and a class which sells its labour. Thus standards of living and opportunity in society are grossly unequal: the latter class have little chance of transforming themselves into the former, either individually or *en masse*. A classless, more equal, more 'happy' society would be achieved by the abolition of the private ownership of large tracts of property, industry and wealth. Industry would be taken into common ownership. The Marxist left believe that to have great concentrations of wealth, and therefore power, in private hands is immoral and undemocratic, as it gives democratically elected politicians limited control over the economy. Industry belongs to the workers who make it productive by the use of their labour power.

There are, however, more pragmatic reasons why a government might seek the public ownership of individual firms or an entire industry. Certainly it was pragmatism as much as ideology which influenced Labour's immediate post-war nationalisations. Labour's 1945 general election manifesto had high hopes for the creation of a more efficient economy through nationalisations, stating:

> Public ownership of. . .undertakings will lower charges, prevent competitive waste, open the way for co-ordinated research and development and lead to the reforming of uneconomic areas of distribution. . .Only if public ownership replaces private monopoly can industry become efficient.

In an industry such as gas or water supply, for example, where the most rational structure might be to have some monolithic body providing the service (as competition would be difficult or impossible), in order to promote control and accountability over that body it could be taken into public ownership. Alternatively a government might decide to take over the largest or most important industries simply to gain greater control over the economy; this was what lay behind the phrase the 'commanding heights' of the economy as a reference to the 1945–51 Labour government's programme of nationalisation. Such control might be exercised on investment and pricing levels, regional development and investment location decisions. For example, if one region of the country is more impoverished than the rest, as were say, Merseyside and the north-east of England in the 1980s, then a company owned by the Government could be forced to locate its next investment there. Whether or not this would be a good thing is a different matter: what matters is the extra control given to the Government by public ownership.

A third reason for public ownership might be crisis management: the taking into public ownership of a company or industrial sector, for a temporary or permanent period, where that company or sector faces obliteration otherwise and where it is considered to be of vital economic, strategic or political importance. The examples from the 1970s are the Rolls-Royce aerospace division,

BL and the shipbuilding industry. A fourth reason might simply be strategic: so that a government has information and control over an important industrial sector, as with BNOC and North Sea oil; or to create a 'national champion' to compete against foreign companies in a sector regarded as being important. The creation of Inmos by the NEB in the 1970s to manufacture microprocessors and semiconductors, where no other domestically based company might have done this, is one example of the latter.

Assessments of the performance of nationalised industries are difficult because guidelines for their objectives were unclear until the advent of the Thatcher governments. Under the Thatcher governments their aims became crystal clear: to make themselves efficient and profitable until they were in a position where they could be privatised. But before this, they were often in the dark themselves about their roles. Were they to be purely commercial enterprises? Or were they to have a wider social role? The provision of employment in economically depressed regions, perhaps? Or the provision of a 'network' of usually unprofitable rural telephone boxes or bus routes? Often, the guidance they had from governments was vague. For a long time, they were told to 'break even, taking one year as against another', without much clarification of what this meant in specific terms. At other times, political interference in their pricing, investment and wages plans has been rampant. In sum, the position of the nationalised industries in Britain was doubly invidious, for they were criticised if they made high profits, being accused of exploiting their monopoly positions, and if they made losses, they were said to be a drain on the public purse.

With privatisation shifting ownership of, and decision-making within, industry back to the private sector in the 1980s, the age of nationalisation may be over unless the political forces of the left can win the ideological debate within the Labour party, and the Labour party can win support from the electorate. Observing the scene in the late 1980s, the combination of both seems unlikely.

But even if the age of nationalisation is over, it doesn't follow that there was never a case for it. In the coal industry, for example, a case could be made for public ownership on the grounds that it would prove safer for mineworkers; research and development could be carried out more effectively under the combined resources of a large corporation rather than being duplicated by 800 companies, and that the dignity of labour could be heightened.

Thus the nationalisation of the coal industry generated enormous optimism among ordinary workers. It was fervently and genuinely believed that a new era of prosperity and security had dawned. Before nationalisation, uncertainty had always been a dominating factor in a miner's life. Piecework wages meant that he feared age or infirmity because his level of pay would fall as his strength to win coal dwindled. The vagaries of free-market capitalism also meant that his very job was uncertain: colliery owners would respond to falls in demand by reducing wages, laying off colliers, or closing pits. Nationalisation, it was believed, would end all this. Security, based on the planned production of an important economic resource, would from nationalisation onwards be the order of the day. As if to emphasise the point, plaques were erected outside each colliery which declared, in heroic fashion, 'This colliery is owned and managed by the National Coal Board on behalf of the people.' Casual working conditions and uncertainty over job prospects were also common in other industries that were later nationalised, particularly the docks and shipbuilding.

Although for most of the post-war era the Conservative party had accepted the existence of the nationalised industries as part of the political consensus, in the 1980s they rejected the idea and their policy was to sell them to private interests. The centre parties at the end of the 1980s, the Social and Liberal Democrats and the Social Democratic Party, also seem to have accepted that the era of nationalisation has reached its end. It is only Labour which is struggling to come to terms with this new age, uncertain whether to clothe nationalisation in a new name—'social owner-ship' encompassing municipal ownership of firms and worker-owned co-operatives, or 'public interest companies', where the government takes a majority shareholding and issues directives to the companies—or whether to attempt to drop the concept altogether and risk the wrath of the left.

NOTE

1. Edwardes, pp. 250–1.

15. Privatisation

Privatisation became the central industrial policy of the Thatcher governments of the 1980s, and looks set to remain so into the early 1990s. It was not an entirely new policy: Mr Heath's Conservative Government of 1970-4 disposed of two state-owned travel agents and the state-owned pubs and breweries in Carlisle during his administration; and, earlier, the steel and road haulage industries were very largely denationalised following the Attlee Labour government's defeat in 1951. Even the Labour government of 1974-9 sold part of its stake in the BP oil company—£570 million pounds worth of shares—as an alternative to further cuts in public expenditure following the sterling crisis and subsequent International Monetary Fund loan in 1976. What was new to the Thatcher administrations was the vigour, pace and enthusiasm with which the privatisation programme was being effected. Up until 1979, the proportion of the economy under public ownership was one of the largest in Western Europe; by the end of three terms of Mrs Thatcher's governments it will have been reduced to a few remnants.

Moreover, privatisation has proved to be a key policy export of the Thatcher governments, with many other countries, in both the developed and less-developed world, following the lead. Canada, Chile, France, Italy, Jamaica, Japan, Malaysia, New Zealand, Singapore, Spain, Thailand, Turkey and West Germany are just some of the countries to have pursued privatisation policies; and some international development agencies have insisted that the condition of supplying aid is that private companies should be allocated the necessary work.

The roll call of privatisations already effected includes the famous and the not so famous, the small and the giant: Amersham International, Associated British Ports, BP, British Aerospace, British Airports Authority (BAA), British Airways, British Gas, British Shipbuilders, British Steel, British Telecom, Cable and Wireless, Fairey, Ferranti, Inmos, Jaguar Cars, the National Bus Company, the National Freight Consortium, Rolls-Royce Engineering, the Rover Group, and the Royal Ordnance factories. The water authorities are to follow before the end of 1989; the electricity industry probably in 1990. In addition, BNOC had its price control and right to buy North Sea oil abolished, and its oil exploration arm sold off as Britoil.

In most cases the state owned the whole of the company, in others, such as BP, British Sugar, Fairey and Rover, they had a large but not always the largest, shareholding. In addition to these central government privatisations, there have been municipal and new town privatisations. The municipal privatisation has included the sale, by the late 1980s, of over a million council houses to occupying tenants, as well as the transfer to private companies of responsibility for jobs the local authorities previously carried out, such as refuse collection, street cleansing, the maintenance of parks and grounds and so on. While some Tory-controlled local authorities had already pioneered these developments, the Local Government Act 1988 forced local authorities, over a phased period, to put these services out to tender and not to act in an uncompetitive manner when deciding which tender to accept: in other words, the obligation would be to accept the lowest tender, which would often come from private companies. In the new towns, as the development corporations which had organised their establishment were wound up, much of the housing, leisure facilities, shopping centres and industrial estates were sold to private investors.

Privatisation, then, refers to a series of related, but different, policies. First, there is privatisation of the *financing* of a service which continues to be provided by the public sector. The debate here addresses itself to whether a service should be financed out of general taxes or from charges made to individual users. By and large the Thatcher governments have favoured the latter, and examples include increased prescription charges and plans to introduce loans for students as a supplement to grants.

Secondly, the provision of certain services has been shifted to the private sector from the public, whilst the financing continues to come from taxation. Examples of this include the Government's insistence that health authorities seek private tenders for catering, cleaning and laundry services, business running into hundreds of millions of pounds; and the transfer of the management of Royal Naval dockyards to commercial, private contractors.

The third, and for our purposes, major, form of privatisation has been the denationalisation of companies. In some cases nationalised concerns were sold to their managements and/or workforces, as in the case of the National Freight Consortium, certain British Steel subsidiaries, and Leyland Bus; in others, state-owned companies were simply sold to other private companies such as Inmos to Thorn EMI, Rover to British Aerospace, and the individual yards of British Shipbuilders; in others still, stock market flotations were organised with vast advertising campaigns aimed at getting as many people as possible to apply for shares. This latter course was the most high profile and its notable—and heavily subscribed—flotations included British Telecom, British Gas, BP and British Airways.

The fourth type of privatisation that can be identified is the liberalisation of markets previously restricted to state or local government monopolies. This allowed private companies to get a foothold in markets previously dominated by nationalised concerns, until the latter themselves could be privatised. The intention of this move was to sharpen competition in order to improve the companies' efficiency and improve services to the consumer. The 1980 Transport Act ended the then state-owned National Bus Company's monopoly over coach routes over 30 miles long. The Transport Act 1985 lifted all restrictions on companies offering bus services, except for certain safety commitments, thus ending local government-run service monopolies in towns and cities. Under the British Telecommunications Act the Secretary of State for Trade and Industry can, and has, with the licensing of Mercury, license companies other than British Telecom to operate telecommunications systems. That Act also gave the government power to suspend the Post Office's monopoly of letter delivery. In energy there has been liberalisation as well: restrictions on private generation of electricity as a main business were lifted in the early 1980s, and following privatisation early in the 1990s, anybody will be able to generate and sell electricity.

What, then, have been the Thatcher governments' reasons for this vast privatisation programme, which netted £5 billion a year in the late 1980s? A series of reasons can be identified, but at the outset it is as well to make some general observations which set the political context within which the programme was pursued.

First, as the party of capital and business, with close links to the Confederation of British Industry, and with a high proportion of business people in its ranks, the privatisation programme could be viewed as simply an expected policy response to a natural constituency. But when one considers that previous Conservative administrations did little to alter the boundaries between the public and private sectors, one realises that there must be more to it than this. Marxists used to argue that privatisation represented an attempt by the Conservatives to open up new business oportunities in the context of the recession of the early 1980s. The fact that the economy was in rapid growth by the mid- and later 1980s, with company profitability soaring, and yet privatisation continued, reduces the persuasiveness of that particular argument.

Secondly, it is possible to consider the right to hold property, which has deep roots and is a central tenet of faith within Conservatism, as a backcloth to the Government's arguments for privatisation. This is important because it is the right of the individual to hold property which underpins many of the other strands of Conservative thinking: the right to inequality, for example, and the right to inheritance as a method of preserving the status quo and maintaining a stable, hierarchical society. The long-held commitment of Conservatives to a property-owning democracy is particularly relevant as far as council house sales are concerned; and it will be noted that the right to buy has not been extended to tenants of the private sector as wider ownership in that instance would conflict with property rights for the individual, which are held supreme. Another aspect of this idea is that property is seen as a bulwark against possible future socialist advance: people will hesitate to vote for a socialist party if they have, as it were, 'something to lose'. Ian Gilmour has propounded this thesis,[1] and it has even led the hard-right Norman Tebbit to champion the idea of worker co-operatives, often associated with the left in politics, where they aid privatisation.[2]

These contextual points made, the Thatcher governments' case for privatisation, according to David Heald and David Steel, writing in the *Political Quarterly* in 1982, could be summed up under four headings: economic freedom; efficiency; wages and pay bargaining; and public sector borrowing.[3] A fifth reason which became important later was wider share-ownership.

According to advocates of privatisation, the existence of publicly owned industry and, in a wider sense, a public sector in the economy, jeopardises economic freedom in two ways. First, the consumer is put at a disadvantage where a nationalised industry enjoys a statutory monopoly or is so dominant in a market that it can act as a monopoly. The sovereignty of the consumer is removed: if a company acts in a way he disapproves of, he cannot take his business elsewhere for there is nowhere else to take it. Secondly, the very existence of a public sector means that members of society have perforce to hold an 'implied shareholding' in that sector, although under different circumstances they might have preferred to hold their wealth in a different form. For example, if British Coal or British Rail, still nationalised at the end of the 1980s, turns in a loss, it is the taxpayer who has to pick up the bill. They could, of course, turn in a profit, thus yielding a 'dividend' to a government, and enabling it to cut taxes, but in either case, the public are dependent on the commercial success of an organisation over which they have no control.

Privatisers argue that we should be free of this thraldom. The logical policy response, therefore, is to encourage policies which foster competition, and to sell public assets and shares so as to reduce the public's 'implied shareholding'. Certain measures have been taken to liberalise certain markets, as I have said, and the 1980 Competition Act extended the terms of reference of the Monopolies and Mergers Commission to include the operations of the nationalised industries.

In practice, however, there have been numerous examples of privatisation conflicting with the fostering of greater competition. The Government, for example, allowed British Airways to take over its main privately-owned British rival, British Caledonian, shortly after it was privatised, thus reducing competition. It refused to use its 'golden share'—one preference share retained by the government in some newly privatised companies, in order to preserve 'last resort' control—to block the take-over of formerly state-owned Britoil by BP, which was again a company in which the government had held a substantial stake. Again, here were two companies operating in the same product area, where their combination reduced competition. In the car industry, prior to the sale of the Rover Group to British Aerospace in 1988, the Government had actively considered selling the company to Ford and was only dissuaded from what would have been another competition-reducing measure by an outcry on its own backbenches.

Opponents of privatisation argued, moreover, that privatisation measures often simply converted a publicly owned monopoly, over which society had some control, into a privately owned monopoly, where the prospects for control were considerably reduced. British Telecom and British Gas are cases in point. The privately owned water authorities will be in the same position, and the privately owned electricity distribution companies will be able to buy their electricity from wherever they wish but the domestic consumer is still likely to have little choice. Admittedly, the nature of these industries makes the introduction of competition a difficult propostion: it would be ludicrous, economically, to have ten companies each laying pipes down a street to supply water. Nevertheless, the key point that opponents of privatisation would make is that a private monopoly will have an inbuilt tendency to use its market strength to increase profits at the expense of the consumer; at least a publicly-owned monopoly can be controlled. Supporters of privatisation argue that regulatory 'watchdog' bodies have been established, like Oftel for telecommunications and Ofgas for gas, to oversee the industries: the counter-argument is that these bodies lack teeth. To summarise, opponents of the Thatcher governments' policy argue that their real priority has been for private ownership, even if this conflicts with liberalisation and increasing competition.

Much depends also on what is meant by 'economic freedom'. Privatisers, in the tradition of the liberal political economists, hold that it is synonymous with minimal government involvement in the economy. Others, however, holding different values, might have different definitions, equating freedom perhaps with a certain standard of material well-being: freedom from poverty; freedom for all, regardless of wealth, to have access to health care, and so on.

Finally, the 'implied shareholding' argument holds only if one believes that private individuals and institutions always take the best decisions from society's point of view, on where and in what to invest. A private company may well, for example, build a luxurious hospital, stocked with all the best equipment and the best-qualified doctors and nurses; the rich would be able to pay for these services, and the company would make profits. But who would provide for the poor, those who can neither afford to pay for treatment themselves nor take out private insurance which would pay for them should they fall ill? It does indeed seem that the National Health Service in Britain is at least one public sector institution in which the population are more than willing to hold an 'implied shareholding'.

Those nationalised industries that existed in the past, and those that remain in the the the late 1980s, cannot go bankrupt or be taken over, as they could if they were privately owned. Advocates of privatisation argue that this insulation from the disciplines of the market bred an inefficiency, a notion among management and the workforce that there was no real need to try harder, to try to improve performance. Nor were managers in nationalised industries, or in the wider public sector, accountable to shareholders who, in a private company where all was not going well, might try to replace the management team. Furthermore, as long as industries remained in the public sector, politicians would be tempted to interfere with their running in pursuit of macroeconomic or macro-social objectives: Ted Heath's Tory administration of 1970–4 restricted price increases in the nationalised industries as part of its anti-inflation strategy; on other occasions, prices have been driven up and factories kept open, against management's wishes. According to privatisers, this type of interference is to the long-term detriment of both the economy and the enterprise involved.

This view of public enterprise sees it as one of a number of institutional structures which have been established during the post-war Keynesian era—examples of others are powerful trade unions and 'high' social security payments—which encourage 'bad' economic management. What were earlier termed social market strategists, the disengagers from the economy, seek to 'unwind' social democracy by dismantling institutions which encourage 'bad' economic management and replacing them with agencies which promote 'good' or 'sound' economic management. Privatisation plays a major role in this: the re-establishment of the situation where it is private individuals and institutions which take economic decisions and therefore determine the nature of the economy.

A problem with this view is that even where denationalisation and liberalisation are brought in as remedies to the alleged deficiencies of public enterprises, the growth in the regulation of those areas of economic activity may mean that the Government, or government agencies, continue to play an active role in monitoring industry. Regulation becomes necessary under three sets of circumstances: first, where there is a direct national security consideration, as for example in the defence or energy industries; secondly, where the profit motive and society's needs are incompatible, as in the maintenance of British Telecom's network of rural telephone boxes or safety precautions in the nuclear industry; and thirdly, to stop a private monopoly abusing its position and exploiting consumers by excessive prices or poor service. The question then arises: if an extensive network of regulation is to continue, albeit in the form of regulatory bodies rather than directly through the nationalised concern, how real is privatisation?

A further potential problem which exists is the phenomenon of 'regulatory capture' whereby the regulating agency comes to identify with the interests of the body it is regulating. Such criticism has been levelled at the Ministry of Agriculture in its relationship with the National Farmers' Union, the representative body of farm owners, and it is a commonplace criticism of regulatory bodies that function in the United States of America.

While a central theme of the Thatcher governments' stance has been efficiency, it is notable that dramatic improvements have taken place in particular companies within the public sector: British Steel was mentioned earlier as an example, Jaguar Cars is another, and the Rover Group returned to profitabilty in 1987–8, within the public sector, doubling the number of cars it produced per man year from 6.9 in 1979 to 15 in 1988. Even the much-maligned British Rail managed an operating surplus of £108.5 million for 1987–8, the best results since the formation of the company, turning round an operating loss of well over £200 million in 1984–5, and raising productivity by 11 per cent between 1982 and 1988. Performances such as these must serve to weaken the Government's argument that efficiency is only possible in the private sector.

Moreover, if increased competition is synonymous with improved efficiency, as may be inferred from government ministers' statements, then the Government faces another problem. The objective of rapid privatisation may conflict with the objective of increased competition. This is so firstly because the smooth transition to the private sector requires the support of the senior management and that support is likely to be given only where the enterprise is not immediately to be subject to heavily intensified competition; and secondly, because investors will be wary of purchasing shares in a company if they fear that its trading prospects will shortly be damaged by an increase in the competition it faces.

The Thatcher government appeared to have several motives concerning pay bargaining which would point to privatisation as an appropriate policy tool. First of all, whereas in the private sector trade unions know that the employers they are bargaining with face a budget constraint—the threat of bankruptcy if wage concessions are too high, where such increased costs cannot be passed on to the consumer—it is argued that in the public sector trade unions perceive that the Treasury will, where necessary, step in to save a company from insolvency. Indeed a Conservative study group chaired by Nicholas Ridley concluded in 1978:

> [Where the nationalised industry trade unions] have the nation by the jugular vein, the only feasible option is to pay up.[4]

The problem of pay bargaining in the public sector has loomed large in Conservative thinking, particularly since Mr Heath's confrontations with the National Union of Mineworkers in 1972 and 1974. Here, certainly, to use Ridley's words, was a union which had the country by the 'jugular vein'. In order to prevent sections of workers from holding the country to ransom, there must, it is argued, be denationalisation and liberalisation. Denationalisation imposes the budget constraints faced by private companies and liberalisation bolsters those restraints as employers find it difficult to pass on higher wage costs as higher prices in the face of intensified competition. It is equally important for a government which does not believe in an incomes policy, like the Thatcher government, to minimise the area within which it has perforce to set wage levels, in the public sector. Hence denationalisation.

The left has also argued that privatisation has been used as a policy tool by the Thatcher government to weaken trade unions, by breaking up the large, public sector trade unions. The central unity of trade unions in the water and electricity industries, for example, will be severed by privatisations which establish several different companies. Privatisation at the level of local government and health authorities—getting private companies to collect refuse, manage sports centres, carry out laundry and catering services—will again weaken unions such as NUPE and COHSE as non-union companies, which can cut their labour costs and thus offer stiff competition, take over.

It remains a matter of conjecture as to whether the existence of budget constraints will influence trade unionists to any great extent in newly privatised concerns. Would the Thatcher government—would any government—sit back and see an important defence contractor, say Rolls Royce, go bankrupt? Governments do, after all, step in to save private companies. It was a Conservative government which in 1971 nationalised the aerospace division of Rolls-Royce, then close to bankruptcy. And it was the Thatcher government itself which intervened in April 1984 by authorising the Bank of England to buy out the bankrupt Johnson Matthey bank. This was, in fact, an extension of public ownership, albeit for a temporary period, as it was sold back to the private sector in 1986 and 1987.

A central concern of the Government has been to take control of, and if possible reduce, public expenditure. High public expenditure was seen as harming economic performance because it meant high taxes, which choked off enterprise and discouraged hard work, or government borrowing, which was seen as 'unsound' economic management. Receipts from privatisation, running at £5 billion a year in the last years of the 1980s, were a source of funds for public expenditure which came from neither taxation nor borrowing, and the Government took full advantage of them. Indeed, receipts from privatisation in the later 1980s were a contributory factor in allowing it to reduce income tax levels.

The Thatcher governments' aims of reducing public expenditure and initiating privatisation can be seen to conflict, however. For by selling off the prime profit-makers in the public sector, such as Britoil, the electricity industry, British Gas and British Telecom, they were actually denying themselves considerable sources of future revenue. Clearly, it was privatisation *per se* that was the overriding objective. Further, the Government was frequently accused of virtually giving away firms: in some cases, the value of the shares in newly privatised companies doubled as soon as trading began on the Stock Exchange.

What became increasingly important to the Government as the privatisation programme progressed was the wider spread of share-ownership in society. Even if it meant selling shares at below their real value, the end result of an inbuilt share-owning constituency was politically worth it. In most cases of privatisation, although some people held on to their shares, a good number sold them, leading commentators to suggest that it was not so much a new class of share-owners that was being created as a new class of speculators. British Gas, for example, had 4.3 million shareholders at privatisation in November 1986. By November 1988, this was down to 2.8 million. But if the overriding political aim of privatisation was to endear the population to the Conservative party and government, then the creation of speculators was probably as good a way of achieving it as the creation of shareholders.

Most of the privatisation of industry that has occurred under the Thatcher governments is effectively irreversible. A future government of a different political complexion would find it almost impossible to renationalise the companies even if it wanted to, which is unlikely given the unpopularity of such a move. But in any case, it is only the Labour party that would wish to renationalise and, at the end of the 1980s, their prospects of forming a government by themselves appear remote: they would need an electoral swing away from the Tories higher than that which they gained in 1945, when the time was right for Labour's brand of collectivism in social and health policy, and when there was a broad consensus on the necessity for nationalising industries to rebuild the economy. Privatisation marked a specific end to an era and stands as a conspicuous testament to the Thatcher years.

NOTES

1. Gilmour (1978), p. 150.
2. The *Financial Times*, 15 February 1984.
3. Heald and Steel.
4. This unpublished report was leaked to the *Economist*, 27 May 1978.

16. Multinational Corporations and Inward Investment

Multinational corporations (MNCs), sometimes called trans-national corporations (TNCs), are companies that operate across national boundaries. Such operations are not just restricted to sales, however, they usually have some deeper involvement such as production facilities in various countries. For them, the entire world is a market; national boundaries do not exist except where they are barred from operating by communist countries, and even there their expertise is often called upon. It was Fiat, for example, the Italian multinational, which provided the designs and much of the original equipment for Lada motor car production in the Soviet Union and FSO production in Poland.

The spread of the multinational corporation is a relatively modern phenomenon. Effectively, their rapid growth belongs to the post-war era, although there are, of course, some examples going back a long time, such as the British East India Company which dated from 1600. They have given rise to the growth of the worldwide commodity, very often American-based, which may be the McDonalds hamburger, Coca Cola or the Ford car. Where national cultures were once dominant in what we wore, ate and drank, now more of us across the globe eat and drink the same. Even beer has not escaped this multinational crusade: Australian lager, usually brewed in the country of its consumption, appears to be especially ubiquitous in the late 1980s. Indeed, it is probably not overstating the point to say that what is being witnessed in the late twentieth century is the creation of a multinational culture, a homogeneity of marketing and consumption spanning the globe.

But it is mainly in the realm of economics rather than culture that the arguments for or against multinationals rage. For the right in politics, multinationals and the concomitant inward investment in Britain are generally regarded as a good thing, although even some right-wingers take exception if it is one of the 'great British industrial institutions' which is under threat from takeover by a foreign multinational, as the Rover Group appeared to be from Ford in the late 1980s. The left is far more circumspect, indeed only the institutions of the City rank alongside multinationals in the hierarchy of socialist demonology. Rarely do they let an opportunity pass of criticising the multinationals. They are said to be guilty of various crimes including anti-trade unionism, environmentally destructive behaviour and exploitation of Third World countries.

Under the Thatcher government, inward investment by multinational corporations has been warmly encouraged. A survey undertaken in 1987 by the Invest in Britain Bureau, an arm of the Department of Trade and Industry established in 1977 to encourage inward investment into Britain, showed Britain to be the major recipient of foreign investment in Europe. Thirty per cent of Japan's total investment in Western Europe came Britain's way, and 36 per cent of the USA's investment in the European Community.[1] One of the most high-profile investments by a foreign multinational in Britain was Nissan's arrival in the north-east. As at October 1988, the total investment, including £125 million in grants from the British government, was £615 million, the largest project by any Japanese manufacturer in Europe, and scheduled to yield an output of 200,000 vehicles a year by 1992.

If multinationals have both economic and cultural effects, they also affect the economic culture. Many multinationals, especially those from the USA and Japan, have brought their own systems of industrial relations and management organisation with them. This often means single-union, no-strike agreements at plants, or no unions at all. As domestic companies struggle to compete with them, they will have to adopt similar practices, thus spreading the phenomenon throughout the economy. Whether or not one thinks this is a positive aspect to multinational investment depends upon one's political standpoint, whether one believes union strength is to be welcomed or cut, and whether one is used to being a member of a powerful trade union that has won benefits for workers.

Large sections of the British industrial economy, and many famous names within it, are in fact owned by foreign multi-nationals. In August 1988, 10 per cent of the UK's workforce, over

1.2 million people, depended on the top 1,000 foreign-owned companies for their jobs. The combined turnover of these companies was £246 billion, and pre-tax profits were £7.78 billion.[2] Since then there has been further foreign investment. Famous multinationals manufacturing in Britain include Ford, General Motors, Lotus (owned by General Motors), Peugeot, Nissan, Daf, Renault, IBM, Rowntree and Courage. Multinationals have a massive share in Britain's North Sea oil industry: in 1988, US companies controlled 40 per cent of our remaining oil reserves, and UK companies had just under 40 per cent.

Multinational investment is, of course, a two-way process. The total direct investment by British companies abroad was £91 billion over the ten-year period to December 1987. This was greater than foreign companies' investment in Britain, which totalled £49 billion over the same period.

The key issue, of course, is whether these multinational operations are a 'good thing' for the British economy. The right are in little doubt. For them, international investment is the corollary of international trade; free trade and the free market are essential to economic buoyancy, and therefore multinational activities are viewed positively. They provide jobs for people, but they also encourage the more rapid diffusion of the most efficient technology and the most efficient management techniques into the economy. Other, possibly domestically owned, companies have to imitate those management techniques and introduce the most efficient technology if they are to survive, and therefore the whole economy benefits. The Nissan investment could be taken as an example of this. Nissan started with a greenfield site, and could design its technology and production and management techiques from scratch and for optimum efficiency. Other domestically based car producers now face a new competitive threat from this 'British' manufacturer, and will have to adapt or face annihilation. Elsewhere, multinational capital can develop an industrial sector that may otherwise have had its development delayed: one thinks of the North Sea oil industry where huge capital sums were required. John Butcher, Minister of State for Industry, summed up their positive effects in December 1987, by arguing that they acted as a spur to competition in the British economy. This was 'a key ingredient in an efficient economy [which] encourages enterprise, more efficient production methods, better management, higher standards of design and quicker responsiveness to changing consumer demands.'[3]

A large section of the left in Britain do not share Mr Butcher's optimism. For them, the ability to control the economy is central to the economic task of a government. Relying on the free market to allocate resources, investment, and to regulate employment, is not enough. Multinationals represent the highest, most advanced, form of capitalism. As such, they represent a threat to the economic sovereignty of a country and its government. Economic sovereignty here means a government's ability to exert some significant control (total control would be impossible except in a completely closed, centrally planned economy) over its own economy, over prices, investment, employment, and so on.

As for the claim that inward investment by multinationals produces jobs, many are suspicious of the quality of these jobs. Multinationals are often accused of effectively turning Britain into a 'screwdriver' economy, in which all the research and development is done elsewhere, with just assembly operations in Britain. And, they point out, there is no way in which Britain could continue to be an advanced industrial economy if this 'screwdriver' sector were to become dominant. Assembly operations can just as easily be carried out in the Third World, with far lower labour costs. Many of the parts used in the assembly could also come from abroad, creating few jobs elsewhere in the economy. Moreover, it is argued, at the first sign of a world trade recession, the multinational company would close down the assembly plant and retreat to its home base, which could be America, Japan or elsewhere. Britain would be left with nothing: no jobs, and no technical expertise to rectify the situation. The Chrysler Corporation of the USA is cited as an example. Facing heavy losses both at home and abroad, Chrysler abandoned its European operations in 1978, selling them to Peugeot-Citroën of France.

But again the right rebuff these arguments; they are the arguments of pessimists who have no faith in the British workman and the British economy. John Butcher said in December 1987 that half of the 322 foreign multinationals surveyed by the Invest in Britain Bureau had research and development operations in Britain. The idea that a great number of plants were just assembly operations, using parts from abroad, was simply 'not true'.[4]

For Stuart Holland, Labour MP for Lambeth Vauxhall, writing in *The Socialist Challenge* and later in *UnCommon Market*, the deleterious effects of multinationals are more widespread. For a start, the operations of multinationals produce inflation. Multinationals, he argues, are often in an oligopolistic situation. In other words, there are just a few companies supplying a particular commodity. In practice, however, they frequently collude and act as a single monopolist. Monopolies can abuse their market position and this is obvious to organisations dedicated to the pursuit of profits to the extent that multinationals are. Thus multinationals charge higher prices for their commodities than would be the case in a free, competitive market.

Even where they do not act in this oligopolistic fashion, Holland argues that they are often 'price leaders' because of their strong position within the market. In other words, if a multinational decides to increase or alter its prices, other companies will follow suit, so as to avoid destabilising the multinational's oligopolistic power and therefore their own positions. For if these companies did not follow the lead of the oligopolistic multinational, they could be destroyed in any price war which might follow.

A second form of economic power wielded by MNCs is in the area of transfer payments: they can 'cook the books'. The most usual form of this is to tell one country that profits have been made in a second country, and to tell that second country that profits have been made in a third country. It is by these means it is said, that multinationals avoid tax and, in certain cases, damage a country's balance of payments. This can occur when a multinational has a large share in a nation's economy—say in a Third World country—and its operation in that country buys components from another sector of the same corporation in another country at inflated prices. These inflated prices can make the country's balance of payments figures appear far worse than they are, thus undermining other foreign investors' confidence in its economy and eventually the value of the currency.

The value of a currency, like the value of anything else in a market-based system, is decided by the laws of supply and demand. Where the confidence of investors in a currency falls, investors will sell and this will depress the price. Where confidence is high, the tendency will be for the value of the currency to rise. Multinationals have enormous funds at their disposal, and like any other prudent investor they want the highest return. They often act, therefore, as speculators in currency, and where they invest their funds, and where they remove them from—for economic, political or strategic reasons—will have an effect on the currency used both in and outside the economy.

Holland also argued that the operations of multinationals remove the option of manipulation of the exchange rate as a policy tool for national governments. While the exchange rate, or the external value of sterling, is no longer 'fixed' at a particular rate, and is allowed to find its own level in the market, this 'float' is, in fact, managed. The Government monitors the rate, and may use other economic levers, such as manipulating the interest rate, to make sure it does not get too high or low. But, it is said, these policy options are weakened by the operations of multinationals. Take the country that engineers a devaluation of its currency in order to boost its exports. If, for example, a car-manufacturing multinational does not reduce the export price of cars manufactured in the devaluing economy by the full amount, then the policy desired by the government cannot be effective. This could well happen, as multinationals fear that by reducing the price of, say, a car manufactured in Britain but sold in France, they would render uneconomic their manufacturing plants in France, which might be unable to match the lower price of the British car.

Holland summed up the threat to a nation's economic sovereignty as including

> the undermining of fiscal and monetary policy; the partial eclipse of exchange rate changes as an instrument of trade policy; exchequer loss, balance of payments cost and inflationary pressure of transfer pricing; and the blackmail of multinational location if they are not allowed the regional location in Britain of their choice.[5]

If these are some of the problems, then what do the left propose in order to control these marauding tigers of capitalism? Some have proposed nationalisation, but this would probably be ineffective and present more problems than it could hope to solve. For a start, it would be likely that whatever was nationalised would be only one very small part of a worldwide production process, probably devoid of any research and development facilities, possibly devoid of any marketing facilities. Short of import curbs against the offending multinational, it would have to compete against its former parent company, and would probably be unable to do so. More importantly, it would sour the climate for other foreign investors completely, and all further multinational investment would be located in competing economies. Others suggest attempting to control multinationals by controlling the economic environment: high taxes on the products they produce might well keep them out, for instance, if that is what is wanted. Allowing trade unions legal privileges might do the same, although they might damage domestic business at the same time. Tax breaks on investment here would probably entice them in.

The control of multinationals is, in fact, one area where the European Community can, and has begun to, play a useful role, in co-ordinating Community countries' responses to investment propositions from multinationals. In the absence of co-ordination, or with only weak co-ordination, when a multinational has declared its intention in the past to invest in Europe there has followed a mass scramble among governments to offer grants, loans and locations to attract the investment. Governments at national, regional and local level attempted to outbid each other, and the only real winner was the multinational itself. And, given that the single market will be in place by 1992, it is access to Europe that is important for the multinational, rather than access to a particular country. The importance of European-wide decision-making procedures therefore intensifies. By the late

1980s, the development of a comprehensive and equitable framework by the European authorities, providing guidelines for the provision of state aid to multinationals, was a priority. State aid which distorts competition in the Community is in any case illegal. To end the competition for multinational investment between member countries would, of course, require the Community to overcome the national political pressures for aid to encourage that investment. It would also have to overcome the sometimes ingenious means of disguising such aid. It may not yet be cohesive enough to make that possible.

The only realistic economic management option for any British government therefore is to continue to encourage multinationals to invest in Britain. Were they stopped from doing so, they would only invest elsewhere in competing countries. They do, after all, produce jobs, and they do have large amounts of capital to invest. The danger of Britain becoming a 'screwdriver' economy should be watched, but it is unlikely that that sector would come to predominate. It should not be forgotten that there are a number of British-based multinationals which would be most likely to keep a substantial amount of their research and development here, but there are also other sectors where we can retain an economic lead, such as financial services.

NOTES

1. The *Financial Times*, 10 December 1987.
2. The *Guardian*, 2 August 1988.
3. The *Financial Times*, 10 December 1987.
4. The *Financial Times*, 10 December 1987.
5. Holland (1975), pp. 198–9.

17. Enterprise Zones

It was in 1977 that Peter Hall, Professor of Geography at Reading University, first canvassed the idea of creating 'mini-Hong Kongs' in Britain as a means of reviving the economy. His was a radical vision: these mini-Hong Kongs would emulate the free enterprise economy of the Crown Colony; there would be few if any restrictions on what businesses could do, in terms of the level of wages they paid, the goods or services they traded in, the way they protected, or did not protect, their workers from hazards in the workplace, the way they developed the land. Taxation would be abolished.

Hall's thesis was that it was partly as a result of the rise of free-enterprise economies in places such as Hong Kong, Singapore, South Korea and Malaysia, that parts of Britain had suffered economic decline—in particular some of the inner-city areas, whose economies had been competing with the newly industrial-ising economies—and had lost out—in industries such as textiles. Hall's argument was that these areas of Britain could not hope to compete against Far Eastern economies which enjoyed much lower labour costs and had been freed, or had never 'suffered', government interference in their workings. Thus Hall envisaged the creation of these mini-Hong Kongs near or in inner-city areas; it would be a bold new departure in urban regeneration policy. He even thought it might be possible and desirable to encourage immigrants from Hong Kong into these new havens of enterprise.

He described his vision in the *Financial Times* in 1984 as being

> a radically different regime, outside the scope of UK customs or legislation, with free movement of labour and capital: a genuine mini-Hong Kong in some derelict corner of the London or Liverpool docklands, representing an experimental alternative to the mainstream British economy.[1]

When Hall first put forward his ideas, Sir Geoffrey Howe, then Shadow Chancellor, took them up with some enthusiasm. The plan fitted in well with the Conservative party's vision of a thrusting, dynamic, free-enterprise economy liberated from the dead hand of state interference. And on taking power, an attempt was made to put a version of the idea into practice. Initially, eleven such enterprise zones, as they were called, were created in 1981 under provisions allowed for in the 1980 Local Government Planning and Land Act. These were in or near the most derelict parts of inner city areas in Clydebank, Belfast, Newcastle/Gateshead, Hartlepool, Wakefield, Speke (Liverpool), Dudley, Corby, Swansea and the Isle of Dogs. A second round of fourteen further enterprise zones was announced in December 1982; by 1988, 26 were operating in Britain, providing employment for about 60,000 people.

These zones, however, were far removed from the mini-Hong Kongs Hall had dreamed of. Howe's plan would not encourage immigrants into the zones, nor would the welfare state be abrogated in the areas. And it was felt that it would be impolitic to lower health and safety requirements or to remove the provisions of the Employment Protection Act in the zones.

Instead, the enterprise zones were to last for ten years, and provide the following benefits to businesses for that time: exemption from rates on industrial and commercial property; exemption from development land tax; 100 per cent allowances for corporation and income tax for capital spending on industrial and commercial buildings; exemption from industrial training levies and from the need to supply information to industrial training boards; simplified planning procedures with concessions on the development that would be allowed; greater speed in dealing with the remaining administrative controls; fewer government forms to fill in; and certain customs facilities processed as a matter of priority.

Hall was disappointed. He expressed his regret in the *Financial Times* article mentioned above, arguing that:

> These incentives are strangely reminiscent of the traditional clutch of regional incentives that have operated in the assisted areas since 1945.

He was particularly disappointed that although planning controls had more or less been lifted in the zones, 'other controls, as on health and safety, remain'.

The Thatcher government's objectives in the creation of the Zones were to encourage the creation of new businesses, attract footloose investment, and help create a new spirit of enterprise. Thus any analysis of the enterprise zone policy has to address the following questions. Have new businesses been created? Have jobs been created that otherwise would not have existed? If jobs have been created, what has the cost been? Have enterprise zones fostered enterprise?

If the creation of employment was a central goal, it must be said that there was no differentiation between types of businesses setting up in the enterprise zones: the benefits applied to all, regardless of whether they were capital- or labour-intensive. Given that the major subsidies available in enterprise zones related to local authority rate and development land tax exemptions, it was always likely that it would be businesses requiring a lot of floorspace that would be attracted there: car showrooms, stock-holding businesses, supermarkets or warehouses. None of these is particularly labour-intensive, although supermarkets might be marginally more so than the others. A survey published by the Department of the Employment in October 1986 revealed that about half of the companies that had located in the Zones were involved in distribution, services or transport. Zones at Gateshead, Dudley and Rotherham, for example, have led to the growth of large shopping centres rather than the development of industry.

Moreover, if the soaking up of unemployment in inner-city areas was a goal, then scant regard seems to have been paid to the type of labour which exists in and around most of the enterprise zones and its suitability for the type of jobs created. Workers frequently had limited education and limited white-collar experience. Any new jobs created were therefore often filled by highly skilled commuters or people moving into the area and buying expensive property that locals could not afford: the Isle of Dogs is the classic example. The complaint of locals there is that the area has been 'yuppified' taking property prices out of their reach and there has not even been the compensation of jobs, which have gone to outsiders. Many of the second-round enterprise zones were not, in any case, near inner-city areas.

In the absence of local authority rates, it was always likely that demand for land in enterprise zones would increase, sending rents sky high and nullifying the original benefit to businesses and at the same time making profits for landlords and landowners. Indeed, on discovering that English Industrial Estates was deliberately asking high rents in enterprise zones to find out what level the market was prepared to accept, the *Sunday Times*, a newspaper usually sympathetic to the Government, was moved to comment in an editorial of 5 July 1981:

> Did the Government, which prides itself on its knowledge and trust of the market, realise this would happen? If so, will the end product be worth the vast amount of public money being spent in rate rebates to firms in the zones—an amount which will increase yearly as sites get developed? If the Government did not expect this, it is an elementary and expensive error.

A more serious condemnation of enterprise zones, if the creation of employment was one of their key objectives, is that companies have merely *relocated* to them, providing a sort of musical chairs of job opportunities, with no net gain to employment in the economy as a whole. Reviewing an early report from the Roger Tym Partnership, which monitored the enterprise zone experiment for the Government, the *Financial Times* of 18 October 1983 had this to say:

> Tym found that nine out of every ten entrants [to zones] had come from the same county. Three-quarters of the companies moving into the zones confessed that they would not have looked outside the county for new premises and an overwhelming 85 per cent said they had no intention of going outside the region.

The conclusion that has to be drawn is that many of the businesses setting up in enterprise zones were simply local firms moving to take advantage of a rates holiday, neither creating any 'new' jobs nor stimulating very much industrial or regional mobility.

The most successful enterprise zones appear to be those that have benefited from *other* government policies or factors extraneous to the orginal enterprise zone concept. For example, the Isle of Dogs, Clydebank and Swansea zones have been particularly successful; the Isle of Dogs attracting an increase in employment of 321 per cent and Clydebank of 105 per cent between 1981 and October 1986 respectively. But the fact is that the Isle of Dogs benefited from the role of the London Docklands Development Corporation, a public body established in 1981 to redevelop the docklands; and Clydebank and Swansea benefited from the much longer-established government agencies, the Scottish and Welsh Development Agencies. Thus the success of these three zones sounds less like the success of a new flourishing spirit of enterprise and more like good old-fashioned government inter-vention.

The Corby enterprise zone was another of the more successful ones. And there again, much of the groundwork for development had commenced before it became an enterprise zone. Corby, a new town, had relied heavily on the British Steel Corporation's plant there for employment and had been economically devastated by its closure. That closure did, however, facilitate sizeable grants in British regional aid and from the European Community; Corby was also well situated in terms of access to London and the markets of the West and East Midlands. Terry McGrain, of the Corby Development Corporation, was quoted in the *New Statesman* of 20 August 1982, as saying:

I think many of the companies would have come here anyway. Associated British Foods, for example, get their cereal crops from the Norfolk and Lincolnshire areas and have their finishing mills in Birmingham. Corby is ideally situated. They would have come anyway.

The cost of jobs created in the zones also appears to have been high. Jonathon Talbot, who has carried out research into the Tyneside enterprise zone (at 1,100 acres, the biggest one of all), noted in *Planner*, February 1988, that loss of revenue which would have come to the Government as taxes, reimbursement of rates to local authorities, and infrastructure development, amounted to about £43 million by the end of 1984. This, he estimated, meant a price tag of between £25,000 and £50,000 per job in the zone. Even the Secretary of State for the Environment, Nicholas Ridley, said on London Weekend Television's 'The London Programme' in May 1987 that the policy had been an expensive one that had not given value for money. In December 1987, he told the Commons that the Government did not intend to establish any further enterprise zones in England, though proposals for other parts of the UK would still be considered.

Talbot's findings on the Tyneside Enterprise Zone were not encouraging: enterprise, new forms of organisation, had not been fostered. He noted in *Planner* that:

The Enterprise Zone has had no effect on either the rate of new firm formation or the type of new firm found in the zone. . .

The study found no evidence that zone firms were more innovative in respect of product and market development or the introduction of new processes or the organisation of the business.

He argued that enterprise zones may, indeed, have been anti-innovatory.

What appears to have happened is that the subsidies provided in the Enterprise Zone prevented firms from innovating, by rewarding their current production relations. Where the Enterprise Zones have stimulated productive innovation, therefore, is among the competitors of Enterprise Zone firms, forced to adapt to reduced market share.

Freeports were a later extension of the enterprise zone idea. Six were set up in February 1984 at Belfast Airport, Prestwick Airport, Birmingham Airport, and in the dock areas of Cardiff, Southampton and Liverpool. Goods can be imported into them, processed and re-exported free of customs levies and national taxes. Taxes are payable only if goods are sent from the freeport into Britain. But their record has been far from encouraging. The *Financial Times* reported in August 1986 that three of the six freeports were facing a crisis which might lead to one or more of them closing. In the Birmingham and Cardiff ones not a single job had been created.

The key problem in trying to analyse enterprise zones, of course, is that one cannot know what would have happened in their absence. It is possible to suggest that many of the businesses locating in the designated areas would have done so anyway. Certainly many were relocations from very close by. The 'spirit of enterprise' does not appear to have been fostered by their existence, and the jobs that were created appear to have been at great expense to the taxpayer. What appears to have happened is that Professor Hall's original ideas appealed, politically, to the Conservative party, but the practicalities of government meant that an almost entirely different policy emerged. Effectively, what emerged was another form of regional policy dressed in the more respectable clothes of free enterprise.

The zones never had any friends on the left: here they were perceived as yet another attempt to undermine the rights of workers, and one more nail in the coffin of the welfare state. But by the end of the 1980s, they had few friends on the right either, given the way the policy had been implemented. Professor Hall could console himself by arguing that his idea had yet to be tried.

NOTE

1. The *Financial Times*, 22 February 1984.

18. High-Tech Industry

Britain's industrial and economic future must lie in what it is or should be capable of doing better than competing economies. This might mean further expansion of the service industries: education, tourism, insurance, pensions and other financial services. In strictly industrial terms, it should also mean expanding the high-technology industries and 'high-tech' applications within other traditional ones. The continuation of traditional work practices and processes, and traditional industries, will see the British economy increasingly trying to compete against countries where labour costs are far lower, or against countries which have introduced high technology on a large scale.

The term 'high-tech' is a catchall description, used to describe a multitude of industries, industrial sectors, products and processes, or areas for research. Robotics, fibre optics, microelectronics, information technology, space research and the space industry, the development of new and improved materials in areas such as plastics, ceramics, special steels and other alloys, are all forming part of a 'technology revolution' in the way we work and the machines we work with. What binds all these areas together is that they are the industries of the future.

It is axiomatic that the advanced industrial economies which do not make the high-tech connection will have increasing difficulty competing against countries and industries abroad that do. And there is some evidence to suggest that Britain has been 'automating' more slowly than its rivals in the 1980s. A report published by the independent Policy Studies Institute in June 1988 suggested that this might be the case, and that the main reason was lack of skilled engineers to implement, supervise and operate change.

A common complaint has also been that Britain spends far more on research and development in the defence sector than its economic competitors, to the detriment of the civil sector. The military field accounted for 27 per cent of total research and development in 1985, compared with just 4 per cent in Germany and 0.35 per cent in Japan. This spending on defence research probably has few spin-offs for the rest of the industrial economy. A large part of the sum goes on nuclear weapons research, for example, and it is difficult to think of many commercial spin-offs from the design of nuclear warheads. This has long been a complaint of the left: Britain, they argue, still thinks of itself as a great power, hence the high defence expenditure, and this great power legacy is damaging to the rest of the industrial economy. The high research expenditure on defence was hardly justified by the fact that defence activities accounted for only 6 per cent of Britain's gross domestic product in 1985, and just 3 per cent of her exports.

Politics enters the scenario because it is up to the Government to decide what, if any, policies to adopt, to ensure that the high-tech connection is made. Essentially, this is an extension of the old argument for and against government intervention. Obviously, one option is to remain on the sidelines, allowing private companies to automate and move into the high-tech era in whatever ways they choose. The other option is for governments to intervene. As far as technology is concerned, the objective of intervention would be to speed up its introduction, by selective assistance to firms and via the organisation of collaborative structures between, say, universities and private firms. Elsewhere, of course, for social and political reasons, governments might seek to decelerate the run-down of industries.

An argument in favour of selective government assistance to the new technology areas is that for some of them the capital investment will be so high, and the returns from that investment such a long way off, that only multinational enterprises will be able to make the investment. In such circumstances, a country might find itself without a domestic base in a major new industrial sector: it was this thinking that led the Labour government of 1974–9 to set up and support Inmos as a national company under the aegis of the National Enterprise Board.

There are other arguments in favour of government support. In microelectronics, for example, the Electronics Components Industry Federation argued in the 1980s for increased government support because the UK industry had neither a large home market like the USA, nor a captive home market like the Japanese. Both these conditions would help to foster the development of a sound industrial base in whatever sector is under consideration.

Indeed, support for the high-tech sector has been one of the areas where the differences between Labour and Conservative have merely been differences of degree and emphasis, rather than of substance. It was Harold Wilson, for example, who managed to hitch science to socialism and talk about forging a future in the 'white heat of the technological revolution' in the 1960s. And despite its free-market stance, and opposition to government involvement in the economy, the Conservative party's 1987 general election manifesto positively boasted about the Government's support for research and development.

> Government support for research and development amounts to more than £4½ billion per year. It is larger as a share of our national income than that of the United States, Japan or Germany. A country of our size cannot afford to do everything. . . The task of government is to support basic research and to contribute where business cannot realistically be expected to carry all the risks.

For the Labour Party, however, support for technology under the Thatcher governments was not enough. Roy Hattersley, Deputy Leader of the party, argued in 1985 that:

> The Tories have become the latter day Luddites with their emphasis on industry that is not so much low tech as no tech. Their priority is low pay and the substitution of workers for machines.[1]

There is, in fact, an irony about the use of the term 'Luddite', for it is one which the Tories would be quick to throw back at Labour over the latter's apparent desire to preserve the industrial structure of the present, with their constant arguments against the closure of pits, shipyards, factories and so on. Of course, Labour would argue that they would not seek to preserve the past so much if there were immediate alternative jobs available.

The 1980s saw a variety of government schemes aimed at boosting the high-tech sector. In 1988 there was the launch of the Link programme. A series of projects lasting up to six years, with around £420 million in funding from government and industry, Link sought to forge collaboration between academic, government and industrial laboratories. The first five Link schemes, announced in February 1988, covered molecular electronics, advanced semi-conductor materials, industrial measurement systems, eukaryotic genetic engineering and nanotechnology. They were intended to be 'pre-competitive' research projects, where companies involved would be free to go their own way using the technology once the research programme finished. Lord Young's view was that the idea was to 'encourage industry to do something that is fairly unnatural for industry—to work with educational establishments'.[2]

The Government also attempted to strengthen the information technology industry in Britain by the £350 million Alvey research programme. This was a five-year programme, introduced in 1983, and was again an attempt to marshal the resources of industry, government and the universities. One of the projects it worked on was the fifth-generation computer. Alvey was launched, in large part, as a response to widespread fears that the Japanese and US information technology industries were leaving Britain's at the starting grid.

The Thatcher governments were less enthusiastic about space, however. Britain's investment in civilian space projects was running at less than £200 million a year in 1988: France was spending five times as much, the Italians and the Germans were each spending three times as much, even India was spending more. Britian's reluctance to get heavily involved in the space industry has often angered her European partners in the 13-nation European Space Agency (ESA). In September 1987 Kenneth Clarke, then a Minister of State at the Department of Trade and Industry, called the ESA a 'hugely expensive club' with overambitious programmes.[3] It was only at the very last minute that Britain joined an ESA-Nasa collaborative space programme, in April 1988, agreeing to contribute £250 million over ten years—5 per cent of the total cost—to the Columbus space station project. The Government also suffered the embarrassment of the resignation of Roy Gibson, the first Director-general of the National Space Centre, in 1987 when the government refused to commit more money to space. The National Space Centre was established in 1985 to provide a co-ordinated strategy for Britain's space industry in the 1990s.

Kenneth Clarke summed up his view of the ESA's plan to put people in space by the year 2000, dismissively in November 1987:

> I still think I'm right and they are wrong. If these countries want to frolic in space on their own then that's their affair.

Whether he is right or wrong, there can be no doubt that the policy of supporting high-tech industry has been an enduring one. The National Research and Development Corporation, which was merged with the vastly slimmed down National Enterprise Board in the early 1980s to form the British Technology Group, began granting financial support for technological innovation and the exploitation of inventions in 1949. On its election in 1964 after 13 years of Conservative rule, Harold Wilson's Labour government established the interventionist Ministry of Technology (or 'Mintech', as it became known). Frank Cousins was its first Minister, from October 1964 to July 1966, when Anthony Wedgwood Benn took over. The computer industry in Britain was one of the sectors it aided with public money.

The 1970s also saw government schemes to support and encourage the high-tech sector. The Product and Process Development Scheme, for example, was launched in 1977 to accelerate product and process innovations through a subsidy to firms' development costs. The Microprocessor Application Project, launched in 1978, was another Labour government scheme aimed at encouraging microelectronic applications in industry, by retraining engineers and technicians, providing grants for new technology, and publishing its benefits. As I have said the Thatcher government stopped most of the high-tech grants to firms.

From a political viewpoint, the real interest in new technology must relate to what effect it has on the political environment, on the economy, and on the society in which we live. As far as the nature of industry is concerned, it has radically altered some traditional sectors: one only has to look at the effect of new technology in the printing industry, for example, which has cut costs, allowed labour to be shed, and allowed tasks to be merged or made completely obsolete. Elsewhere, it has led to the development of completely new industries: microelectronics is the obvious example.

One predicted effect of the introduction of new technology, with political repercussions, was a reduction in the number of jobs available. So far, however, studies show the effect on employment to have been less damaging than feared. The Policy Studies Institute report referred to earlier showed job losses resulting from automation as being 45,000 a year between 1983 and 1987, and between 15,000 and 20,000 a year over the 1981–3 period.

It was also thought that the introduction of technology would weaken unions: they would lose members, and the workforce would be more difficult to organise as demarcation lines between jobs broke down, and as there was more 'individualised' working from home. As a consequence, it was argued, trade unions would oppose its introduction. But the findings of a research project published in 1987 as a book entitled *Union Structure and Strategy in the Face of Technical Change*, edited by Eric Batstone, Stephen Gourlay, Hugo Levie and Ray Moore, refutes both these claims.

The researchers examined practices across a variety of industrial sectors—brewing, chemical manufacturing, machine spares and the insurance industry—covering 16,600 employees, and found that unions were not weakened by new tecnology, nor did their members, on the whole, oppose its introduction. Batstone and his colleagues came to the conclusion that:

> There is little evidence in our case studies of union influence declining—if anything the reverse—and there is no evidence that the unions were being by-passed in a way which was distinctly different from what had always occurred.

Within the 'politics of industry' there is also a 'politics of technology'. The political and social consequences of a government or society choosing a certain type of technology in preference to another should not be overlooked. In terms of energy policy, for example, the Thatcher governments have been keen to open up the coal industry to the brisk winds of the market place, and cut off subsidies, but less keen to put the nuclear industry under the same pressure. Thus, the choice of a particular type of technology is often a political choice, not merely a technical one. It may be argued, for instance, that certain aspects of the information technology and microelectronics industry represent an 'isolationist' technology, with movements towards shopping from home, working from home using computer terminals, entertainment from home via satellite television and videos, separating individuals and families from the rest of the community. Some would go further and argue that this reinforces an 'individualist' ethos within people and society and weakens any 'collectivist' ideas that may have existed hitherto. For political parties appealing to people as individuals, and others calling for collective provision of housing, education and health, and collective ownership of industry, the consequences are obvious.

NOTES

1. The *Guardian*, 6 June 1985.
2. The *Financial Times*, 4 February 1988.
3. The *Financial Times*, 11 November 1987.

19. Small Businesses and their Promotion

What is a small business? Definitions differ, but essentially, when politicians and economists speak of them they are talking of a business which may range from a window cleaning round to a manufacturing concern employing 200 or 250 workers.

From the point of view of the right, the small business sector has been popular for both economic and political reasons. In economic terms, because the small business sector is often very easy for new people to enter, they have to be competitive to survive. The competitive struggle leads to innovation, which increases efficiency and keeps prices down, reinforcing the battle against inflation. The best small businesses grow bigger, bringing with them jobs. While they stay small businesses, they are unlikely to be strongly unionised, if they have unions at all; and, as we have seen, strong trade unionism is unpopular with the right.

In political terms, the small business sector also appeals to the right. A businessman or woman of whatever stature, they feel, is more likely to vote Conservative; or at least not to vote Labour. They 'own something', 'run something'. They are separated from the rest of the labouring classes by this distinction even if not by education or social skills. All this fits well with the idea of the enterprise culture, with 'every man a capitalist', 'every man a man of property'.

The Thatcher government's analysis of Britain's post-war economic problems placed emphasis on the argument that the entrepreneurial spirit necessary for people to start small businesses had been stifled by the high personal taxation necessitated by high public expenditure and that government regulations of all kinds, such as planning constraints, red tape and employment protection legislation, had choked off potential business activity.

For Mrs Thatcher, the creation of small businesses in Britain would solve unemployment. She told the House of Commons in March 1985:

> [The answer to unemployment]. . .will come about when our people, instead of relying on increased subsidies, do exactly what is happening in the United States and in Japan and set out to create more small businesses themselves.[1]

Small business promotion and encouragement is one of the policy areas agreed on by all sections of the Conservative party. Ian Gilmour, for example, at times one of Mrs Thatcher's strongest critics within the party, has noted that:

> some of the troubles of the British economy since the war surely stem from the fact that many Englishmen have a deficit rather than a surplus of entrepreneurial desires.[2]

It should be noted, however, that not all small businessmen or women are entrepreneurs. An 'entrepreneur' wants to expand business, is fuelled by prospects for further profits. Other small businessmen, running fish and chip shops, motor repair garages or plumbing services perhaps, might just want to earn a steady living. Thus, while in theory, encouraging 'entrepreneurship' *might* lead to a more dynamic, thrusting economy and encouraging small businesses might soak up some unemployment, it could still fail to promote an enterprise culture.

Since the Thatcher government came to power, there have been regular exhortations from leading ministers that the way forward to a brighter economic future is through the setting up of small businesses. The idea is that with the relaxation of legally enforced monopolies in certain industries, such as buses, telecommunications, electricity generation and parcel delivery, competition will intensify and it will be easier for people to enter a previously excluded sector and set up new small, as well as large, businesses. Moreover the downgrading of, and proposals to abolish, wage councils, which set minimum wages for 2.5 million workers in 1989 and the curtailing of trade union power by legislation, both strengthen the position of businessmen and potential businessmen in relation to their employees.

The Government has also introduced more carefully targeted, more specific measures aimed at encouraging people to set up businesses. While there have been some dissenters, many economic commentators have argued that a 'gap' existed in the market in the provision of relatively small sums for small businesses. The most significant policy measures aimed at plugging this 'gap' have been the Loan Guarantee Scheme, the Business Expansion Scheme, and the Enterprise Allowance Scheme. The second Thatcher government also saw the inclusion of Lord Young in the Cabinet, first as Minister without Portfolio and later as Employment Secretary, with a special brief to create a climate favourable to the encouragement and success of entrepreneurship. In the third Thatcher administration, Lord Young moved to the Department of Trade and Industry. In 1985 he published a White Paper *Lifting The Burden*, which charts a course for freeing businesses from red tape and thus stimulating their establishment and development. The lack of a sufficiently robust small business sector is, of course, intimately connected with the absence of an enterprise culture, which Lord Young gives as one of the reasons for poor economic performance in Britain:

> I believe very strongly it is because of our culture, because of the sort of circumstances in the fifties and particularly the sixties and seventies when profit-making, making money, was somehow not quite nice.[3]

A further White Paper of similar vein, *Building Businesses. . .Not Barriers*, followed in May 1986; and another one entitled *Releasing Enterprise* in November 1988. The latter detailed plans for civil servants to be seconded to business, for a simplification of planning regulations and food and drink law, and for a pilot chain of 'government business shops', initially six in number, where business can obtain advice on taxation, employment protection law and government assistance available for business start-ups. In addition, 1985 saw the creation of the Enterprise and Deregulation Unit (EDU), aimed at lifting red tape and restrictions on small businesses. The EDU moved with Lord Young to the Department of Trade and Industry.

It could be argued that the increase in the number of self-employed over the past few years is a consequence of encouragement by government ministers. Statistics show that over the period 1982–5, there was a 15 per cent increase, and the number of self-employed stood at 2.7 million in March 1985. It should not automatically be assumed, however, that there are really so many people literally employing themselves; if that *were* the case it might be a reflection of an emerging enterprise culture, an emergent and robust class of self-employed small businessmen. But the rise in self-employment might simply mean that an increasing number of conventional employers are taking advantage of the savings available to them of having their workers nominally 'self-employed'. Employers can, via this method, avoid having to make a national insurance contribution for the employee, and it is easier to get rid of workers when they are no longer required. Many people in the hairdressing business and the construction industry, as well as people such as driving instructors and taxi drivers, for example, are technically 'self-employed'. Yet it is quite obvious that in reality many of them are selling their labour, in the conventional sense, to an ordinary employer. The 'ordinary' employer continues to own the stock—the hairdressing shop, the taxi cab—and organise and manage the work. In 1987 in the construction industry, for example, there were about 600,000 self-employed workers, compared with 500,000 directly employed by building firms. Many of these 'self-employed' builders are actually directly engaged with building firms. Such a 'technical' change in status allows the worker to claim expenses against tax and the employer to avoid holiday pay as well as the National Insurance contribution. There is little ground for believing that the rise in self-employment marks a nascent enterprise culture, or in less ambitious language, a newly robust small business sector.

The Loan Guarantee Scheme is a measure which has sought to plug the supposed finance 'gap' facing small businesses. It was introduced in 1981, and while it provided an average of 500–550 loans a month during its heyday in 1982 and 1983, the monthly total in and after 1985 fell to only about 100–150. The scheme did not fulfil the Government's optimistic hopes for it, although it continues to operate. Its function was to guarantee repayment initially of 80 per cent of loans up to £75,000 from banks to small businesses, in return for a premium of 3 per cent on the guaranteed amount paid. In 1984 the Government's guarantee dropped to 70 per cent and the premium was raised to 5 per cent of the amount guaranteed. There have, however, been two major problems with the Loan Guarantee Scheme. First, right from the start it has been enormously expensive for the small business borrower. Because of the increase in the premium charge, and the fact that the banks have usually charged between 1.5 and 2.5 per cent over the base rate on guarantee loans, an LGS loan in December 1984 would have cost a business between 20.5 and 21.5 per cent in interest charges. In an effort to alleviate this problem, the 1986 budget reduced the premium from 5 per cent to 2.5 per cent.

Estimates published in May 1983 by the London and Scottish Clearing Banks suggested that the Loan Guarantee Scheme was accounting for between 3 and 4 per cent of total lending to smaller businesses and around 1 or 2 per cent of new facilities. The logical conclusion can only be that the Loan Guarantee Scheme has played a very minor role in the provision of finance to small businesses, and it has probably had no effect on the promotion of an enterprise culture. The second problem of the Loan Guarantee Scheme has been the expense to the Government of a business's failure to repay or bankruptcy. The *Financial Times* reported on 1 April 1986 that banks participating in the scheme had claimed a total of £119 million from the Department of Trade and Industry, and it appeared that bankruptcies amongst firms with guarantee loans were running at 40 per cent.

The Business Expansion Scheme (BES) was started in 1981, as a successor to the Business Start-up Scheme. It operates by allowing investors to buy shares in unquoted companies and claim tax relief on such investment, at whatever income tax rate is applicable, providing the investment is held for five years. Each investor can invest up to a maximum of £40,000 and still qualify for tax relief. Thus, if an investor pays income tax at the standard rate of 25 per cent and invests £1,000 under the BES, his total outlay will only be £750 as the rest will be refunded. Obviously, the higher the investor's tax bracket, the more attractive the scheme becomes. An investor paying 40 per cent income tax would only have to find £600 for the same £1,000 investment.

The March 1988 budget extended the BES to those engaged in buying and renting property as a business, and limited the amount that could be raised by any BES to £500,000 a year in an attempt to ensure that it was *small* businesses that benefited from the policy.

The Business Expansion Scheme had several objectives. In a similar fashion to the share-flotation privatisations, it was intended to encourage a new class of equity investor. It was also to be another means of providing finance to smaller firms which otherwise would not have been able to find it. A survey has shown that about a third of companies receiving money under the BES thought they would not have obtained the finance elsewhere. Figures for 1983–4 show that about half of the companies receiving money were new start-ups, and the smaller enterprises —the ones which have the greatest difficulty obtaining relatively small amounts of finance—had benefited significantly.[4]

Its success has not been total, however. The scheme's contribution to the creation of an enterprise culture has at best been very limited indeed. It is a fact that few 'ordinary' men and women in the street have heard of the scheme, and many businessmen are also unaware of it. It is mainly the people who are keen readers of the financial press, or are already involved with financial advisers, in other words, an already existing elite, who have been introduced to it. The people who became involved with the BES would probably have been wheeling and dealing with their money anyway: there has been little or no extension of the entrepreneurial franchise. And yet the thrust of the Government's rhetoric in this connection is that the option of starting a small business, of becoming part of the enterprise culture, should be open to all.

A second somewhat negative aspect is that instead of being perceived by those involved as having the primary function of promoting commercial and industrial enterprise, the BES has been seen very largely as a tax shelter for the well heeled in one of the industries that has always shown signs of robust health: the tax-avoidance industry. Furthermore, evidence shows that BES investment has been disproportionately channelled into the south-east of England, probably the area of Britain already closest to having an enterprise culture anyway.[5]

The Enterprise Allowance Scheme (EAS) was introduced nationwide in August 1983. It provides people who have been unemployed for a minimum of eight weeks, or under notice of redundancy for that length of time, an allowance of £40 per week for a year if they start a business, providing they can find £1,000 themselves. The intention of the scheme is to encourage the unemployed to find the solution to the problem by employing themselves, and to alleviate the initial cash flow problems of doing so. Moreover, it aims to create a new class of businessmen and women and in that way make a contribution to the bringing about of an enterprise culture. Whether it can be judged a success or not depends upon the criterion of assessment: the results seem to have been mixed. On the positive side by January 1986, 126,000 people had been helped into self-employment. Some 86 per cent of those helped were still trading three months after the allowance finished.

On the negative side, however, the only alternative to the EAS for many people in the depressed areas seemed, for a long time, to be unemployment. Alan Humble, director of Hartlepool Enterprise Agency, which helps people getting involved with the EAS in one of the most depressed parts of the country, said in March 1988:

> The vast majority here now look to the EAS out of desperation to escape unemployment or because they cannot think of anything else to do. Some are seduced by the advertising and hype and don't understand the implications.[6]

There is a sense in which it may be argued, therefore, that the scheme represents a kind of covert coercion of people who want to earn a living into gambling on possibly risky business ventures. Furthermore, many of those people now operating under the EAS might have been doing the same thing in the black economy anyway in an effort to keep their costs to a minimum, even if the scheme had not been established. If this is the case, it means that the overall contribution to economic activity in the country produced by the EAS is much smaller than might appear at first sight. Moreover, studies in the mid- and late 1980s showed a drop-out rate from the scheme of one in eight, though many of these are people finding alternative jobs. Such a rate may not be particularly high, but it emphasises the point made earlier that a proportion of those entering the scheme have not suddenly thrown off the wage-labour tradition and developed an entrepreneurial mentality: it is just that the alternative was often the dole.

Some of the projects being financed were also criticised, with people signing onto the EAS as musicians and with similarly dubious projects. Indeed, it began to look as if the EAS was being used by local Job Centre officials as simply a means of reducing the unemployment figures in a particular locality.

A key strand of the Government's approach to the creation of an enterprise culture in which small firms can flourish has been the much trumpeted cutting of red tape and the deregulation outlined in Lord Young's *Lifting the Burden, Building Business. . . Not Barriers* and *Releasing Enterprise*. In addition to the removal of certain government regulations, the need to fill in official forms, and all the other red tape that is supposed to be frustrating entrepreneurial activity, *Lifting the Burden* provides for 'simplified planning zones' which exempt businesses from having to seek permission for most development, in much the same way as existing enterprise zones. Again, however, the argument that such measures will help to promote a robust enterprise culture is open to dispute. A survey carried out by civil servants in 1985, for instance, supported the line that, in reality, there was no grass-roots pressure for deregulation at all, just a small number of vociferous pressure groups calling for it.[7] In addition the argument that cutting red tape will encourage small businesses is a catch-all explanation. It fails to explain why, when all firms face the same kinds of regulation, the proportion of small firms in some industrial sectors—timber and furniture, metals, clothing and textiles for example—is at least equivalent to comparable countries, while in other areas, such as food, drink, and tobacco, it is smaller.[8]

Before the Thatcher era governments tried to pursue policies aimed at small business promotion; the Small Firms Service, for example, was set up by the Heath government in 1972–3, to provide information to small businesses through a network of regional offices. There have also been attempts by private sector banks in the 1980s to help small businesses. The Thatcher government, however, invested a good deal of political capital in this area. Partly this was an attempt to soak up some of the unemployment of the 1980s, but mainly it was part of a wider attempt to change the political environment: an attempt to broaden the property-owning, business-owning class, and so to entrench support for the Conservatives. Whether it was a policy investment worth making on economic grounds is open to dispute.

NOTES

1. House of Commons Official Report, Vol. 74, Sixth Series, Session 1984–5, p. 775.
2. Gilmour (1983), p. 28.
3. The *Guardian*, 20 March 1985.
4. The *Financial Times*, 7 May 1986.
5. The *Guardian*, 24 December 1985.
6. The *Financial Times*, 15 March 1988.
7. The *Financial Times*, 18 January 1985.
8. *British Business*, Department of Trade and Industry, 19 November 1982.

20. Local Authorities and the Economy

The deepening north-south divide of the late 1970s and the 1980s, together with the rejection by the Thatcher governments of active involvement in the economy, prompted some local authorities to engage themselves in much more robustly interventionist policies in their own local economies. Many local authorities of different political complexions had, since the inter-war period, pursued what can be called a 'traditional' approach to industrial development in their areas: they had provided sites for industrial development, for example, or premises in which businesses could locate. In the 1970s, these 'traditional' approaches began to expand. Local authorities began to advertise their town or city as a potential location for businesses in magazines and on billboards, aiming the advertising at key private investors; they sent delegations of councillors or officials to world trade conferences; they lobbied central government and the managements of large companies either to invest more or not to withdraw investment, not to close a particular plant or factory; some provided loans and grants to businesses. Very often, councils appointed industrial development officers at a senior level to co-ordinate these activities.

But the 'new' and radical activities of some local authorities in the 1980s were intended to break away from what were seen as ineffectual gestures, and they were also designed to deal with much more severe problems. The West Midlands, for example, which for much of the post-war era had been regarded, along with the south-east of England, as one of the most prosperous areas in the country, was hit very badly by the economic recession of the late 1970s and early 1980s. The 'new' activities were also far more politically symbolic, reflecting the rise of the 'new urban left' within the Labour party which criticised past Labour government policy as well as that of the Conservatives. This new urban left, in effect, began to capture the local political machinery in many of the urban areas: the actual personalities involved were often a 'new breed' of Labour councillor, better educated and in white-collar occupations, displacing the more conservative, community-oriented, old guard stalwarts who had been Labour's contingent since the war. The new urban left had new ideas, and wanted to put them into practice. Given that Labour lost elections nationally in 1979, 1983 and 1987, they very often saw themselves as the real opposition to Mrs Thatcher's governments. Some, like David Blunkett of Sheffield, Ken Livingstone of the former Greater London Council, and Margaret Hodge of Islington, became famous along the way.

The majority of councils did something during the 1980s to stimulate their local economies. A survey conducted in 1985 of the largely Conservative-controlled district councils in the non-metropolitan areas revealed that, out of the 76 per cent who responded, only 11 per cent did not undertake economic development work. Much of this was the provision of premises, sites or advice. The new urban left in the metropolitan areas, however, went much further than this. Sheffield City Council set up an Employment Department in 1981 to take on an active, interventionist role and co-ordinate economic development activities in a city ravaged by job losses in the steel industry. Following the Labour victory in the May 1981 West Midlands County Council elections, an Enterprise Board was established to pursue similar activities on a larger scale. That board survived the abolition of the metropolitan county councils in 1986, as did an enterprise board established by the Greater London Council. After Labour regained control of Lancashire County Council, Lancashire Enterprises Limited was launched in 1982, making profits of over £2 million in the period to 1987. Greater Manchester County Council launched an Economic Development Corporation in 1979. This corporation, which was taken over by the ten boroughs which formed Greater Manchester when the metropolitan county council was abolished, saw profits of £1.6 million in the financial year 1986–7. Merseyside and West Yorkshire County Councils also launched enterprise boards.

In addition to the political symbolism of the new approaches, they also reflected the perceived inadequacies of the 'traditional' economic development initiatives. Much of the locational promotion work that formed part of this traditional approach, for example, was seen as a 'beggar-my-neighbour' policy, merely relocating employment from one place to another. The encouragement, assistance and advice given to small businesses, often a major plank of traditional approaches, also came under fire from those who argued that it could be up to 25 years before such a policy bore fruit in terms of increasing employment. It was big and medium-sized firms, they argued, that had shed the jobs. It was towards these that new policies should be directed. The financial incentives offered by local authorities to indigenous and international firms simply resulted in a Dutch auction; each authority would try to outbid the others, and the only beneficiaries would be the companies themselves.

The new enterprise boards and economic development units decided that instead of trying to attract new firms to their areas, they would concentrate on the indigenous firms and, in particular, on the medium-sized and large ones. One of the problems facing these companies was seen by the supporters of these initiatives as a lack of sympathetic investors, and the short-term nature of lending by traditional financial institutions, compared with those of Japan or West Germany. Most of the enterprise boards at least paid lip-service to the idea that if the company had no chance of long-term success, there was little point to this local government intervention.

Most of the enterprise boards, as a *quid pro quo* for loans and investment, also wanted some sort of agreement with the individual companies on how they would develop their businesses. In some cases, this would be an agreement to develop particular products and employ a certain number of people. In many others, it included trade union recognition and some broader commitment to the rights of employees, as well as an agreement to employ a certain number of people from the ethnic minority population. These were as much 'social' as 'economic' policies. Some authorities developed these social policies further by insisting that any companies the authority dealt with, for building projects, or the supply of soap, office equipment, overalls and so on, conformed to certain requirements, such as recognition of trade unions and the employment of people from ethnic minorities. Some, such as Lewisham, even went further, refusing to deal with any company which had links with South Africa. (This ban was overturned in the courts.) These conditions became known as 'contract compliance', and the Local Government Act 1988 effectively outlawed them.

The enterprise boards and economic development units were therefore intended to play an active part in their local economies. They would not sit back passively and wait for lame-duck companies to come knocking at their door, they would actively research their local economies seeking out companies and industrial sectors which needed restructuring, financial assistance, new premises or land, or help of some other kind. The development of equity investment in companies was seen as particularly important by some, especially West Midlands Enterprise Board, allowing major expansion to take place in companies without saddling them with heavy debt, as well as providing long-term investment for the board. Most of the new urban left saw their creations as being models for what a future Labour government could do on a national scale.

Sometimes the 'traditional' activities, such as lobbying, continued alongside these new approaches. Thus Sheffield City Council, in alliance with trade unions and South Yorkshire County Council, launched a 'Save-Our-Steel' (SOS) campaign in 1983 to lobby both the British Steel Corporation and the Government. Sheffield had seen unemployment treble between 1981 and 1984, to the point where it stood at 45,000 in March 1984. The aim of the SOS campaign was to prevent the merger of the BSC River Don operations with the nearby, privately owned Firth Brown, to create the new Sheffield Forgemasters, and the job losses that would ensue from that. A publicity campaign was launched, with advertising on buses and billboards, and delegations were sent to see relevant government ministers and industrialists. Though it may have succeeded in heightening awareness of the problems in the steel industry—though awareness was pretty high anyway—it failed to stop the merger and the job losses.

Much of the funding of the enterprise boards and economic development units has come from Section 137 of the 1972 Local Government Act. This allows for local authorities to spend a sum 'up to the product of 2p in the rate' for purposes in the interests of the community. As the restrictions on local authority spending have been successively tightened by central government, enterprise boards have begun to look further afield, to pension funds for example, for financial support. With the replacement of domestic rates by the new community charge in 1989 in Scotland and 1990 in England and Wales, the prospects of funding continuing from the public purse look uncertain.

What, then, have been the results of these local authority endeavours? Attempts at measuring success usually aim to evalute how many jobs have been created and at what cost. Lancashire Enterprises Limited claimed to have created 6,900 jobs between 1982 and the end of 1987, at a cost of £2,900 each.[1] Greater Manchester Economic Development Corporation claimed, by advancing loans and investment totalling £3 million, which in turn attracted £30 million of private sector investment, to have helped to create 4,300 jobs between 1979 and 1987.[2] West

Midlands Enterprise Board claimed that it had helped create 2,000 jobs in its first two years of operation, 1982–4; and that the £5.53 million of public money invested in that period attracted almost £23 million of private investment.[3]

Attempts to analyse these initiatives in this fashion, however, are unsophisticated. It is true that the growth of particular companies in a local economy can have beneficial 'knock-on' effects: expanding companies might take up more supplies from other local companies, increasing jobs there, and the extra purchasing power in employees' pockets would benefit other local businesses such as shops. These sorts of evaluation procedures, however, are less than complete. What are the wider ramifications of assisting particular companies? The expansion and progress of one firm, bringing increases in employment, may simply mean the contraction of a competitor company, and therefore a decrease in employment, either in the locality or further afield. Moreover, the question returns to the usefulness of financial assistance to firms from governments of whatever type, local or national. A study was carried out in the early 1980s on companies which had been given loans or grants by Tyne and Wear County Council. Employment had increased in these firms by 967 jobs (81 per cent). The author finds, however, that of these 'only 182 were jobs which in the opinion of the owner/manager of the firm would not have been created without aid from the local authority.'[4]

Other critics of local authority intervention argue that, although they claim to have 'saved' jobs, what they have really done is preserve the status quo for a little longer and delayed necessary change.

At best, what local authorities can achieve in terms of local economic development is a limited, but marginally beneficial, role in regeneration. At worst, local authority intervention can degenerate into a form of political posturing, where 'heroic' councillors seek to experiment in their local economies, making political appointments at officer level along the way to carry out the tasks. The wider question is whether local authorities should have any role whatsoever, beyond the fairly innocuous advertising of the location and the provision of industrial sites. Those of the liberal political economy tradition, for example, would completely reject the 'new' economic strategies of the new urban left: they are one more example of governments 'meddling' in the economy with harmful results.

NOTES

1. The *Financial Times*, 29 October 1987.
2. The *Financial Times*, 2 December 1987.
3. Action in the Local Economy. Progress Report of the Economic Development Committee, WMCC.
4. D. Storey: 'Local employment initiatives in north-east England: evaluation and assessment problems' in Young and Mason, p. 202.

21. Europe and Industry

The way people in Britain perceive Europe appears to be changing, albeit gradually. The European Community is still viewed as being some kind of vast, nebulous, bureaucracy 'out there'; the turn-out in elections to the European Assembly continues to be at the low level associated with local government elections; and few people would be able to recite which countries are members of the European Community, let alone name their Euro-MP. But there does, nevertheless, appear to be a growing acceptance that Britain's rightful international place is within the Community. The sight of Jacques Delors, the President of the European Commission, addressing, and being applauded at, the 1988 TUC Conference would have been nothing less than astonishing a few years earlier when an array of trade unions were bitterly and actively opposed to continuing Community membership. The extensive advertising campaign organised by the Department of Trade and Industry in 1988 to make people and businesses aware of the single market to be introduced from 1992 has also raised the profile of Europe.

But despite this apparent mass indifference, among those deeply involved in politics the question of whether Britain should remain a member of the European Community has been bitterly contested. Many on the left saw, and still see, the European Community as a 'capitalist club', a supranational state designed to bolster capitalism across Western Europe and defeat any socialistic tendencies in member states. The European Community, it is believed, would thwart any attempt to implement a left-wing economic strategy, which might include nationalisation, controls on the import and export of money and goods, and financial assistance to companies and industries. Thus, in much the same way as the multinationals and the City, the European Community represents a threat to the 'economic sovereignty' of a country such as Britain.

Most of the right and centre-right, however, are committed, in varying degrees, to the idea of the Community. There are sections of the 'libertarian' right, though, those more closely associated with the perceived need for free trade and free markets who are still hostile. Enoch Powell, for example, has argued vehemently against it. For him, the European Community represented a governmental body which intervenes in markets, as with agriculture, and which also represents a threat to the sovereignty of the British national parliament.

The European Community was, to start with, three communities. The six founder members, France, West Germany, Belgium, Luxembourg, Italy and the Netherlands, formed the European Economic Community in 1958. For countries which had been ripped apart by war with each other little more than a decade earlier, such a union could only be welcomed. The European Coal and Steel Community was also formed in 1958, as a recognition of the importance of those two industries to Western Europe in strategic and economic terms. Euratom was also founded in 1958 to foster collaboration in the civilian sector of nuclear power. It was in 1967 that the three communities were merged and they became known, collectively, as the European Community. Since the original union, six further members have joined: Britain, Ireland and Denmark in 1973; Greece in 1981; and Portugal and Spain in 1986.

What, then, of collaboration in industrial affairs in the Community? Should some kind of Euro-policy on industry even be considered? Agriculture has always had a high priority, accounting for about three-quarters of the Community's budget. Policies on industry have had a much lower profile. There are some strong arguments in favour of industrial collaboration, and even some arguments to support a common industrial policy monitored and implemented on a European-wide scale. The first argument for greater European industrial collaboration is the straightforward one that companies and economies within the Community would obviously benefit from the pooling of talent and resources spread across half a continent. The argument then turns on whether some kind of government involvement, at national or European level, is necessary to bring this into effect, or whether it would happen naturally as private sector companies realise the benefits to be gained. The right has argued against involvement.

The second reason for collaboration is connected with the first. It is that European-wide initiatives will have to take place if the economic 'threat' of the Americans and the Japanese is to be countered. A third reason advanced is that the nation-state as a unit within which political decisions can be taken is obsolete, or is at least being made so by multinational companies and financial institutions that operate as if national boundaries did not exist. It is argued that the only way to stop multinationals from hawking their investment proposals around various countries in search of the highest bidder, which benefits only the multinationals themselves, is to respond on a pan-European scale. Others argue for a greater European element in industrial policy simply on the grounds that their ultimate goal is a federal Western Europe, a complete economic and political union on the model of the United States of America. In a country still fairly uninterested in the Community this argument is unlikely to carry much weight.

There are, in fact, a number of collaborative industrial projects at the European level. March 1985 saw the European Community announce Brite (Basic Research in Industrial Technologies for Europe). Brite was a transnational programme involving 432 firms, universities and research institutes across all of the twelve member countries. It had Community funding of £80 million over 4 years, and was aimed at projects designed to help the Community's traditional industries, such as chemicals and car manufacture, become more competitive with those of Japan and the USA. It followed the model of a joint public–private initiative, with the consortia involved expected to match the £80 million government funding. Brite was granted more European money for a second phase to run from 1988 to 1991.

Another programme, known as Esprit, was approved by the Community in February 1984. Esprit, the flagship of the Community's industrial research programme, was a £471 million five-year project, again bringing together companies and research institutes across the Community in an effort to create a competitive European capacity in information technology. Esprit was seen by its supporters as acting as a catalyst to pre-competitive research by companies in different Community countries. Half the cost of research initiated in this way was paid by the Community, the other half by the companies themselves. Such research might not otherwise have taken place according to advocates of Esprit, without this governmental 'spur'. Moreover, they say, projects such as these avoid duplicating effort and give a European scale to research. A second phase of Esprit, with European funding of £1.1 billion, was announced in December 1987.

A further project, launched at the end of 1985, which had eighteen participating European countries including six outside the EEC, was Eureka. Eureka was the brainchild of the French, who were committed to the state-funding of projects, and was again aimed at the high-tech sector. Again the focus of attention was the need to compete with the US and Japan. France's idea was that co-operation would be achieved across the whole of Western Europe, stretching beyond research into marketing collaboration and, in the meantime, avoiding the delaying politics and bureaucracy of the European Community. The first ten projects announced in November 1985 under the aegis of Eureka were concerned with microcomputers, compact vector computers, solar power, robotic lasers, membrane microfilters, high performance cutting and welding lasers, seeing robots, medical diagnostic kits, data collection on airborne pollution, and computer network research.

Collaboration between Community countries has also taken place in nuclear fusion and space. Britain's reaction to many ideas for collaboration in the 1980s, however, has usually been to welcome the efforts on the condition that no governmental money was involved, and this often caused friction with the other member states.

One area in which there was an element of success in devising a European industrial policy was in the steel industry. As it approached the 1980s, it was clear that the steel industry in Western Europe, as in the rest of the world, was facing massive problems of overcapacity. The British Government had its own solution which entailed a dramatic slimming down of the British Steel Corporation (BSC) under the stewardship of Mrs Thatcher's personal appointee as Chairman, Ian MacGregor, who took over the job from Sir Charles Villiers in 1980. Sir Charles had, in fact, already laid the foundation for the closure plans before MacGregor's arrival, and had also effectively broken the resistance to plant closures by the Iron and Steel Trades Confederation and the other steel unions by stewarding the Corporation through a 13-week pay strike in early 1980 which resulted, to all intents and purposes, in a defeat for the workers.

The BSC was established as a nationalised corporation in July 1967 by the Iron and Steel Act of that year. It became the sole owner of the shares of fourteen companies which had produced 475,000 gross tonnes or more of steel in the year ended 30 June 1964. Its establishment at that time represented the largest ever industrial merger in the United Kingdom. In keeping with the mood of the times, the strategy envisaged was very much one of restructuring and expansion, fostered by state intervention and encouragement.

The BSC's first development strategy concentrated on exploiting the potential of the five major steelworks that it had inherited. These were the so-called 'heritage' works of Port Talbot, Llanwern, Scunthorpe, Lackenby and Ravenscraig. This ten-year plan, after modifications by the Heath administration, was outlined in a White Paper in February 1973. It proposed that each of these five plants should be brought up to its optimum capacity and modernised. Additionally, it proposed a new steel works on the south bank of the River Tees and held out the possibility that two smaller electric arc steelworks might be constructed. The BSC's capacity would thus be increased to a maximum of 36–8 million tonnes in the early 1980s. In actual fact, production in 1984 stood at 15.14 million tonnes; by 1987–8, it was producing about 14 million tonnes.

This projection and subsequent outcome highlights the problems of planning in a capitalist economy. Planned or socialist economies are not inherently superior—in the majority of ways they are patently inferior—but it has to be said that capitalism is subject not just to the minor booms and troughs of the business cycle, but also to periods where there is a high optimism for economic growth and other periods of severe retrenchment.

Thus, there was a decline in employment in the BSC from 230,000 in 1971–2 to 94,000 in October 1982. In the early 1980s, the process of job-shedding gathered momentum, with a total of 65,900 jobs being lost between January 1980 and May 1983. By December 1987, the BSC employed only 51,200. In the preceding seven years, 80,000 steelworkers had lost their jobs, and a further 30,000 had been transferred to private sector companies forged out of BSC subsidiaries.

Within the overall context of this massive job-shedding, two tendencies served to compound the problems caused. The first was that steel closures were taking place in areas already suffering from high unemployment, such as the north-east of England and Scotland. The second was that they were also taking place in areas where the steel industry had been the dominant employer and therefore the mainstay of the local economy, as at Shotton in North Wales, Consett in County Durham, or Corby in Northamptonshire.

Other European countries faced similar problems, though Britain was the first to go through massive retrenchment. It was announced in October 1987, for example, that 34,900 jobs would be lost in the West German steel industry up to the end of 1989. France and Belgium had also been particularly badly hit.

Despite the fact that Britain would have slimmed down its steel industry anyway, this was one area where the European Community did take a hand, imposing a mixture of controls on imports of steel, production quotas and minimum prices. The intention was to give the industry a chance to restructure itself within the Community, without engaging in a damaging price war for the then dwindling number of consumers.

The ability of the Community to formulate a common policy on steel was probably due to three factors: first, the fact that the steel industry was in manifest crisis and that crisis affected all of the major industrial powers within the Community; secondly, the wider powers given to the European authorities by the European Coal and Steel Community, and thirdly the leadership qualities and the determination of the European Commissioner responsible for the steel industry, Viscount Davignon. Similar attempts to formulate a common policy on shipbuilding failed to make much headway.

There were some problems in the implementation of the policy, however, especially over the allocation of quotas for production. For while it was the European Community Commission (the 'civil service' of the Community) that set the quotas in broad national terms, it was left to Eurofer (the 'club' or business group of European steel makers) to translate how the quotas should be distributed between each particular steel product. In July 1983, Britain and France were awarded quotas slightly more generous than they had previously been, as a reward for rationalising their industries, but the other members of Eurofer were extremely reluctant to go along with this agreement. As a sanction, the Community has imposed fines on steel companies, but these can be difficult to collect. The West German steel company, Kloeckner-Werke, simply refused to join the quota system until 1984, by which time it had accumulated a total of £40 million in fines. The British Steel Corporation itself has also deliberately exceeded quotas at times and faced fines. For companies trying to build goodwill amongst customers, there is understandably strong pressure to put the customer first, regardless of governmental pressures to do otherwise. In June 1988, it was announced that by the end of that month, the system of quotas was to be abolished. Privatised in November 1988, the British Steel Corporation would therefore face the future as a privately owned company operating in free-market conditions.

An analysis of European steel policy highlights one of the most serious obstacles to the development of a common European policy on industry, should one ever be desired: nationalism. Western Europe is comprised of old nations, with old languages and old, separate cultures. The Germans, French, Italians, Spanish and British look to their own countries first and to Europe only second, if at all. Domestic politicians have to win power, and face elections, in their own country; it is they, not Europe, that are held to account for the state of the economy and society. Nationalism is a powerful political and social force; it cannot be submerged or diluted within a matter of a few years.

And the countries which suffer from 'competing' nationalisms, such as Northern Ireland or the Basque region of Spain, are more painfully aware of that than anyone else. As long as political power remains at the level of nation states, the determination of overall policies for industry will remain there too. And until the development of a 'Euro-society', in which people identify as closely with Europe as with their own countries—which may never come—political power will always remain at the level of the nation state.

There are other problems that would have to be overcome by the advocates of a common European industrial policy. First, although it is not insurmountable, there is the problem that the people of Europe speak many tongues, unlike the people of the United States of America. By designating one language for communication, say English or French, the worst effects of this can be overcome, but the fact that there are many languages does not help matters. Secondly, the member states of the Community are at vastly different stages of development: policies for Greece and Portugal, for example, might simply be targeted at promoting industrial and economic development; policies for Britain, France and West Germany, on the other hand, are more likely to be focused on bringing about a transition in the economy from older, traditional industrial structures to high-tech and service sectors. Moreover, the dominant political forces within the member countries might well be opposed to each other: could a socialist Greece negotiate successsfully over policy towards industry with a free-market Britain? Essentially, of course, these are problems that have always dogged the Community. It took ten years, for example, to agree a common fishing policy, and it has argued for many years about the size of the budget and about the common agricultural policy.

In practice it is likely that the industrial policy that is pursued at the European level will settle down to the promotion by the Community of a few high-tech projects, some voluntary co-operation largely between private sector companies, as has happened in aerospace (with subsidies from some national governments); and the strict maintenance of a free-market environment within which companies have to operate. After all, although there are some provisions for exceptions, the principle of the free market is enshrined in the Treaty of Rome which set up the original Communities, with Article 92 stating:

> Save as otherwise provided in this Treaty, any aid granted by a Member State or through State resources in any form whatso-ever which distorts or threatens to distort competition by favouring certain undertakings or the production of certain goods shall, in so far as it affects trade between Member States, be incompatible with the common market.

So perhaps, as the left argue, the Community really is a 'capitalist club'. Opposition to it on those grounds alone, however, would only be justified if one believed, that capitalism is to be condemned *per se*. Marxists will believe that, but others will not. Certainly, it is in the maintenance of the free market that the Community has most often bared its teeth. The European Commission has banned aid to the textile industry, for example, a restriction upheld by the European Court of Justice in November 1987 after an appeal by the French. And from 1987 onwards, national governments cannot give aid to their domestic shipbuilders at a rate of more than 28 per cent of the cost of a particular contract; the Commission told the French government in February 1988 to cut its aid to the shipbuilders Chantiers de l'Atlantique by FFr100 million, on an order by Brittany Ferries which had been placed there at the last minute in preference to a yard at Govan in Scotland.

Those committed to a federal Europe will continue to argue for more collaboration on industrial and economic policy; indeed, they will press for economic and political integration. But the prospects, or at least the prospects of Britain being part of it, look slender at the end of the 1980s. The British have always been somewhat reluctant Europeans. As at 1988, they are still not members of the European Monetary System, the mechanism for stabilising currency exchange rates of which all the other member states are members. Britain's protest over the size of her budgetary contributions dominated European political affairs between the summits of Dublin in November 1979 and Fontainebleau in June 1984, preventing progress on other fronts.

Mrs Thatcher's position on federalism was very clear. Speaking in September 1988, she said that plans for political integration or federal development within the Community were 'airy fairy and absurd'. In a speech in Bruges, she scorned the European federalists.

> Europe will be stronger precisely because it has France as France, Spain as Spain, Britain as Britain, each with its own customs, traditions and identities. It would be folly to try to fit them into some sort of identikit European personality.[1]

And, like Enoch Powell, she saw the Community as a body with a propensity for intervening in, and preventing the unimpeded operation of, the free market. Her response was unequivocal:

> We have not successfully rolled back the frontiers of the state only to see them reimposed at a European level.

NOTE

1. The *Guardian*, 21 September 1988.

22. The Future of Work

If inflation and stagnating economic growth were the key problems facing the British economy in the 1970s, in the 1980s it was unemployment, which reached levels not seen since the 1930s. Unemployment was a problem which stretched across Western Europe, but in Britain it was particularly bad, reaching well over 3 million, or about 13 per cent of the workforce, in the mid-1980s. Unofficial estimates suggested that the real total was closer to 4 or 4½ million, as many were effectively unemployed— married women, school leavers, men over 60—but unable to register for benefits.

But the distribution of unemployment was uneven. There were always many more jobs available in London and the south-east of England than elsewhere and the places that were most badly hit by unemployment were areas which had relied on the old, possibly obsolete, industrial structure: the north of England, Scotland, Northern Ireland and large parts of Wales.

Arguments rage as to *why* unemployment reached such peaks in the 1980s, with the left blaming the Thatcher governments for deliberately stoking it in order to enervate the trade union movement; and the right responding by blaming the world recession of the late 1970s and early 1980s, together with the trade unions who, they said, prevented the markets for labour from working as they should.

As evidence that unemployment would be an enduring

problem, commentators also cited the trend that seemed to be apparent in many industrial and commercial sectors towards the replacement of labour by machines, robotics or applications of microelectronics. That trend was said to be continuing and accelerating, to the extent that opportunities for employment in the traditional sense would be much more limited in the future. What is undoubtedly true is that many large industries in Britain shed employees on a huge scale during this period—engineering, steel, shipbuilding, coal and car manufacture for example.

As unemployment grew theorists emerged who argued that there might, in future, be a large, permanent 'pool' of unemployed people; that society might have to rethink its traditional assumption that work for all would continue to be the norm; that the 50-week, five-day week model of work might have to be discarded as the available work was shared out more equally. All these theorists assumed that the world was entering a new phase, a phase in which there would be changes in patterns of work, lifestyles and production.

'Deindustrialisation' entered the language as one description of what was happening to areas of Britain. Many contended that a 'post-industrial' society was emerging. In general, deindustrialisation was lamented, particularly as little, in terms of economic activity, seemed to be evolving to fill the resultant vacuum. Yet there were also grounds for optimism, for a post-industrial society might provide the basis for human emancipation. The radical writer Ivan Illich, for example, considered that:

> A post industrial society must and can be so constructed that no one person's ability to express him or herself in work will require as a condition the enforced labour or the enforced learning or the enforced consumption of another.[1]

Deindustrialisation also forced Marxists to reconsider their traditional assumptions regarding the working class and the transition to socialism. André Gorz, for instance, commented:

> The crisis of socialism is above all a reflection of the crisis of the proletariat. The disappearance of the polyvant skilled worker—the possible subject of productive labour and hence of a revolutionary transformation of social relations—has also entailed the disappearance of the class able to take charge of the socialist project and turn it into reality. Fundamentally, the denigration of socialist theory and practice has its origins here.[2]

Not everyone shared these visions of the future. Lord Young is on record as saying in the mid-1980s:

> I do not accept for one moment all those prophets of doom and gloom who talk about a world in which there will not be full

employment, in which there aren't sufficient jobs to go around, into which we are going to have to start training people for leisure. All those prophets in the past have been proved wrong.[3]

Charles Handy, in his book *The Future of Work*, argued in 1984 that full employment as it has been known in western societies has gone forever. His thesis is that in the future manufacturing, for example, like agriculture in the twentieth century, will produce wealth but few jobs. From a left-wing perspective, the trade unionist Clive Jenkins and Barry Sherman, in *The Collapse of Work* (Eyre Methuen, London, 1979), pointed to what they saw as a paradox. For many, they argued, work is a chore, seen as being an unpleasant necessity. And yet, on the other hand, the work ethic is so deeply ingrained in Britain and other industrialised societies that work has acquired a value in itself: people feel incomplete if they do not have a job; others in society judge one by the status of one's job; the nature of one's job forms part of one's identity. Jenkins and Sherman postulated that Britain faces a choice as it enters the last years of the twentieth century. The first option, they argue, is for British industry to equip itself as quickly as possible with robotics and microelectronics applications, which would, as the programme progressed, mean that demand for labour would be significantly diminished. The other option is one of resisting technological developments and continuing manufacturing and commercial operations in the traditional way, using the same amount of labour. This would mean, however, that as other countries adopted new technologies, Britain's businesses would become less and less competitive, both at home and abroad. Large-scale unemployment would result as British businesses lost orders to foreign competitors.

Both options, then, would result in far fewer jobs in the economy and, as a consequence, Jenkins and Sherman had no hesitation in proposing the route presented by the first option as the only logical one for Britain. To deal with the resultant labour surpluses, their solution is to propose a leisure revolution in which the available work in the economy is spread out in a more equitable manner. So there would be more part-time working; more workers taking (paid?) sabbaticals; a reduction in the length of the working week and day; and an expansion and extension of education, so that it is no longer seen as something one engages in at the start of one's life. Education, they argued, should be a continuing process, available at all levels and ages.

André Gorz is another influential writer who has expended energy analysing this 'future of work' question. In *Paths to Paradise*, he too argues that the days of full-time, full employment are gone forever. For Gorz, the crisis of unemployment which hit Western Europe in the late 1970s and 1980s was not a temporary interruption but a *consequence* of economic growth. The thesis is that past economic growth produced full employment which in turn produced labour shortages as expanding companies could not find enough workers. In these circumstances, machinery was increasingly introduced as a substitute for labour, in order to maintain economic growth, and therefore profitability, in individual enterprises. Full employment also shifts the balance of power in the economy towards the workers: they can demand, and win, higher wages and better conditions, thus imposing further costs on the firm. The pressure to automate as a substitute for labour is obvious. This, for Gorz, is the root cause of the crisis of unemployment of the 1980s.

Like many Marxists, Gorz sees the politics of conspiracy in operation. He argues that politicians in the 1980s were pretending that full employment was still a norm that could be returned to, in order to preserve the existing form of social relations between employers and employees. In other words, he believes that the capitalist ruling class's domination of workers can continue only so long as work is the employees' main occupation. Where that is the case, their dependence on their employer comes to dominate their lives. If, however, work became merely one activity amongst many, as it might do if there were a 'leisure revolution', this domination would be destroyed. The labour force would no longer passively accept the decisions or power of the employers. The world Gorz imagines being created in this new 'liberated' phase brings to mind the famous passage from Marx's *The German Ideology*:

> In communist society, where nobody has one exclusive sphere of activity, but each can become accomplished in any branch he wishes, society regulates the general production and thus makes it possible for me to do one thing today and another tomorrow, to hunt in the morning, fish in the afternoon, rear cattle in the evening, criticise after dinner, just as I have in mind, without ever becoming hunter, shepherd or critic.

Marx is in one of his excessively romantic moods here, yet the point he is making is clear, and is expressed more prosaically by Jenkins and Sherman.

> What is so special about work and is it arranged properly over an individual's lifetime? Is it not ludicrous to slave away week after week, year after year and only have a large block of leisure precisely the time we need it least and can use it least—at retirement?[4]

If the future is going to be one of large-scale unemployment brought about by technological advance, or some other reason, and the only solution *is* a leisure revolution, then there will be related economic, political and sociological problems that have to be overcome. If people have a *need* to work, for example, to give them an identity, convey social status, provide a place to form friendships, and so on, then there would have to be a substitute for this social role of work. As a means of overcoming the social isolation felt by the unemployed, Gorz suggested an expansion in what he called the 'politics of collective facilities': by this he appears to mean that some kind of community centre could be set up in every town, city or apartment block, offering a forum where people can meet, drink tea or coffee, swim or partake of other sports, carry out repairs to machinery they have, or read books from a library. These centres, he believes, would form an alternative focus for life. As for the 'identity' problem, Jenkins and Sherman postulate that it is capitalism that has inculcated the idea that it is the norm to organise one's life around work, for without wage labour, capitalism itself would have foundered; it would be the role of a new expanded and invigorated education system to dislodge this popular misconception.

There remains, however, the problem of income distribution in this kind of workless society. As long as there was full employment, income distribution may well have been unfair, but it nevertheless existed. If full employment cannot be assumed even as a possibility, the situation changes radically, for two reasons: first, there would presumably be a great number of people without jobs for long periods, and perhaps not at all; and secondly, there would presumably be a great disparity between the remuneration offered for different jobs, thus intensifying tensions in society. For those in high-tech, professional areas, the rewards would probably be high; there would be others, however, in an expanded, part-time, service sector forced to sell their labour, possibly domestic service, maybe even sexual services, to their richer brethren.

To overcome this problem, many of the 'workless future' theorists propose a minimum payment made to all by the state to guarantee a basic, reasonable standard of living. Gorz sees no problem about financing this minimum payment: it would be secured by a tax on the high-tech, automated sector of the economy. As well as raising the finance to pay for the minimum income for all, this tax would prevent prices of goods and services from the automated sector falling, which would also benefit society. For example, if cars could be designed and built by robots very cheaply, it might nevertheless be undesirable from society's point of view for them to *be* cheap. Cheap cars would encourage even greater consumption, using up natural resources (metals and oils), and cause noise, congestion and airborne pollution. Jenkins and Sherman's belief is that there should be no financial penalty to being unemployed: unemployment benefits should be paid at around the national average wage of those in work.

Some 'workless future' theorists appear to believe that perceptions and attitudes will be so different in years to come that the obvious problems of this kind of minimum income payment can be ignored. But politics is about reality, and the reality is that some of these policy prescriptions should never have been allowed to escape from their socialist fantasyland. What of incentives, for example, in this 'workless future'? If someone can get the national average wage for not doing anything at all, why should anyone bother to do the work that needs to be done? The answer, for Jenkins and Sherman, is very basic and very simple:

If the state paid everyone a decent wage, then work could be done by those who wanted to do it. It could be in cooperatives under local authorities, private entrepreneurs or directly for the state, but in all instances, nearly all, if not all of the profits would accrue to the public purse.

If this were the case, where would be the incentive for a firm to innovate or invest? Why should anyone bother to train for long periods for particular specialist jobs? The cost of paying everyone a 'decent' wage would be astronomical, leading to much higher taxation; yet which political party would risk its electoral chances by proposing such a step? Where would the 'private entrepreneurs' come from, if all profits go to the state?

Jenkins and Sherman do point out, convincingly, that if the future *is* to see a large number of unemployed, unless a mechanism can be found for overcoming their alienation from an ever more consumption-oriented society, then such unemployment will be politically destabilising. An 'underclass' cannot be kept under forever without trouble. That trouble may manifest itself as some kind of antisocial behaviour, such as crime or vandalism, or politically as extremist parties of the right or left gain favour.

What is beyond doubt is that if the 'workless' state is an accurate description of the future, then the political ramifications will be manifold. Gorz thinks that it would bring about a loss of employers' power over workers, but it would surely also bring about the loss of trade union power. The power of the unions depends on having workers to organise. The problem for the left is further compounded by the fact that it is likely in the new technological age that people will be able to work from home in much greater numbers: this would mean the end of the factory, the works, the office as social units. It would strengthen the forces of individualism as opposed to the principles of collectivism which form the ethos of trade unionism.

It may never come to this; Lord Young may be right after all. At the end of the 1980s, unemployment in Britain is on the downward trend; moving downwards towards the two million mark at the end of 1988, although in some places it remains very severe. Indeed, rearing its head on the political agenda as the 1990s approach is the concept of 'workfare', an idea imported from the USA where, in some states, the unemployed have to work before they get their benefits. Workfare assumes, as the school of liberal political economy does, that unemployment is essentially voluntary. People are not working because they refuse to work for the (often low) wages that are on offer. To ensure that they are not therefore 'scrounging' from the taxpayer, they should be forced to work. Whether one accepts this view depends upon where one stands on the political spectrum: but what workfare does provide is evidence that, as a society, we have not moved far away from the ingrained work ethic which some would have us believe is the root of all the trouble.

NOTES

1. Illich, p. 13.
2. Gorz (1986), p. 66.
3. The *Guardian*, 26 March 1985.
4. Jenkins and Sherman, p. 6.

PART FOUR
Industrial Case Studies

Case Study 1: The Politics of the Coal Industry

No industry in twentieth-century Britain could rival coal for being politically charged. Here was the 'jewel in the crown' of the 1945–51 Labour government's nationalisation programme; the industry which had produced a string of prominent, politically motivated radicals such as Will Paynter, Dai Francis, Arthur Horner, A.J. Cook and, in the 1970s and 1980s, Lawrence Daly, Mick McGahey and Arthur Scargill. Here was the industry that conjured up evocative visions of pit-head winding gear, of gloomy-looking but happy and resourceful terraced-house communities, of gruelling hard work, of terrible disasters. Here was an industry and a group of workers little understood by outsiders. Its mystique survived the 1980s. How could *anybody* last out on strike for a whole year? How could *anybody* survive that long deprived of their main source of income? People outside the industry were baffled: but the communities' unity and resourcefulness are attributes which stretch back generations and have been preserved in myth and legend in coal-mining areas. And that strike was, of course, one of the key episodes in the 'politics of industry' in the 1980s.

The strike against pit closures in 1984–5 represented a new response to an old phenomenon. Pit closures had, after all, been taking place with varying degrees of frequency since the late 1950s. And while it was the concept of 'uneconomic' pits that lay at the heart of the dispute—the Thatcher government and the then National Coal Board wanting to close them, and the National Union of Mineworkers (NUM) wanting them to remain open—it should be recognised that both Labour and Tory post-war administrations have closed, or threatened to close, pits which were classed as uneconomic or potentially uneconomic.

Throughout the 1950s, the 1960s and most of the 1970s the position adopted by the NUM towards these closures was one of compliance and co-operation with the National Coal Board (NCB) and the government of the day. It was only in the 1980s that this position was changed to one of resistance. Why and how this change came about and why the policy of the NUM for much of its history was one of acquiescence is the subject of this chapter. Unless these questions are examined, the 1984–5 miners' strike cannot be fully understood.

The first essential fact that must be recognised is that though many post-war colliery closures have taken place because of seam exhaustion, the state owners have more often closed down pits because they were deemed uneconomic. This means that the extraction of coal costs more than could be recovered from its sale, or alternatively that coal production was running at a higher level than demand. In the 1950s and 1960s when there was full employment, other collieries were closed simply to release labour for more 'efficient' pits. This happened at the Devon colliery in Alloa, for example, which was closed in 1959 in order to provide labour for the new Glenochil pit, which had opened in 1956.

The dimensions of post-war decline should be drawn at the outset. In 1957, more than 207 million tons of coal were extracted from British collieries. This was down to 178 million tons by 1965. By 1970, it was a little over 133 million tons. By 1975 this had fallen to just 114.7 million tons. And the average level for the 1980–4 period was about 110 million tons. Between 1957 and 1975 the number of collieries fell from 822 to 241, and the number of miners from 704,000 to 245,000. In November 1984 the official manual workforce of the NCB was 189,000, of whom 178,000 worked at 174 pits. From May 1981 to October 1982, 22,000 jobs were lost in the British coal industry. Indeed, the Wilberforce Inquiry, set up to examine the miners' 1972 pay claim during the strike of that year, officially recognised the severity of this contraction, saying:

> The rundown, which was brought about with the cooperation of the miners and the union is without parallel in British industry in terms of the social and economic costs it has inevitably entailed for the mining community as a whole.[1]

Some coalfields escaped relatively lightly, while others were devastated. In general it was the 'central' coalfields of Nottinghamshire, Derbyshire and Yorkshire which were least affected, while the 'peripheral' coalfields, such as South Wales, Durham and Scotland, suffered most. In Nottinghamshire, for example, there were 31,078 miners in 1947. By 1974 this had been reduced by less than a thousand, to 30,300. But in the Durham coalfield, by contrast, manpower fell from 97,924 in 1958 to 44,160 in 1968. By 1974 the number of miners employed in the Durham coalfield was 18,420. Between 1958 and 1968 120 collieries closed in the north-east of England. And in the fabled Rhondda Valley, which once boasted 66 collieries, there remained in 1984 just one—the Mardy. By 1988, the workforce of British Coal (as the NCB renamed itself in April 1986) stood at 117,000, a reduction of 104,000 over the three previous years. However, this figure included management, white-collar and ancillary staff. The number of blue-collar workers must have been less than 90,000.

There are five 'phases' of pit closures that can be identified in the post-war era. The first occurred during the first decade after nationalisation, 1947–57. Before that phase is discussed, it is important to note that nationalisation itself was very largely a bipartisan strategy. The Conservative party, for the most part, accepted nationalisation as an integral part of the post-war economic reconstruction. Though Tories such as Colonel Lancaster, a colliery owner, railed against nationalisation in the Commons as the requisite legislation was going through in 1946, Winston Churchill himself, as Leader of the Conservatives, had told the House in 1943:

The principle of nationalisation is accepted by all, provided proper compensation is paid.[2]

Indeed, the Conservatives' decision to nationalise coal royalties in 1938 formed an important prelude to what was to take place under Attlee's Labour government.

Pit closures within this first decade took place within the context of stable or rising production overall. The Reid Report (1945), written by mining engineer Charles Reid, had provided a technical stimulus to the political forces pressing for nationalisation, and advocated reorganisation and rationalisation. It argued that collieries should be 'merged into such sizes as would provide the maximum advantages of planned production'. Once the colliery owners were out of the way, the NCB set about implementing the Reid Report. Its aim was to eliminate small, inefficient pits in this first round of closures. Thus, of the 980 mines inherited in 1947, there were only 822 left by 1957. These closures, however, by no means affected all coalfields equally. Most miners were untouched by them. In Durham, for example, 1947–57 saw 15 closures, but almost all of them because of genuine exhaustion of reserves. Yorkshire and the central coalfields escaped largely unscathed.

Scotland, on the other hand, faced many closures. The Lanarkshire coalfield was almost obliterated.

It is significant that this first round of 'rationalisation' was started under a Labour administration and continued in the same form after 1951 under the Conservative government. There was no change of policy after 1951. The first rationalisation was a bipartisan policy. Moreover there was no opposition to this round of closures from the NUM. Overall there was a rising demand for coal; in general, there was full employment. The industry had been nationalised, for which the union was immensely grateful, and the Conservative government had not sought to denationalise it, over which they were relieved. From the NUM's point of view, it was of paramount importance to ensure that their sought-after nationalisation was a success and was seen to be a success. If this meant reorganisation, or some mild rationalisation in the interests of the industry as a whole, they were pleased to accept it. In corroboration of this, the miners' president Will Lawther told the annual conference in 1947 that nationalisation meant: 'There are now no opposing sides in the industry.' This stance continued when the Tories took over in 1951.

The second phase of closures covered the period 1957–63. Demand for coal had been rising or stable until 1957 and had given nationalisation an aura of success in its first decade. But in 1957, the first post-war fall in demand occurred. 1956 had seen inland coal consumption reach a peak of 218.4 million tons, but by the year after it had fallen to 213.2 million tons. The NCB at the time apparently considered the fall in demand to be a mere aberration, believing business would pick up as the trade cycle recovered. In reality, however, the events of 1957 were the beginning of the turning point in the history of the British coal industry. After 1957, apart for a brief respite in 1960, the decline in demand for coal continued and established itself as a trend. Between the end of 1956 and the end of 1959 total consumption had fallen by no less than 35 million tons each year. The temporary recovery in 1960 accounted for no more than 8 million tons.

The NCB, under the Tory government, reacted as any rational enterprise does under capitalism when facing falling demand: it closed production units and reduced manpower. Workers in the industry, numbering 704,000 in 1957, were down to 571,000 by 1961. By and large those colliers who wanted to be were re-employed at other pits, though in some cases these were 200 miles away. During 1958 and 1959, 85 collieries employing nearly 30,000 men were closed. By 1963 Britain had 264 pits fewer than it had six years earlier, as a result of this fall-off in demand. Employment numbers in the industry fell by 30 per cent. The real villain of this piece was the emergence of cheap oil. As the price of oil fell relative to coal, coal was allowed to be squeezed out of the market for electricity production. While the price of oil for power stations fell from 2.0p per therm in 1955 to 1.6p per therm in 1960, the price of coal rose from 1.5p per therm to 1.7p per therm over the same period.

Though free-market considerations in fuel policy determined that the domestic coal industry should be allowed to run down, some concessions in favour of coal were in fact made by the Conservative government. In 1961 a duty of 2d a gallon was imposed on oil used for burning at power stations, ostensibly for revenue reasons, but partly in order to protect coal. The electricity industry was asked to stop the switch from coal to oil, and licences were refused for the importation of American coal. But these measures only cushioned the worst effects of the coal rundown. They were by no means a concerted attempt to save the domestic coal industry from severe contraction.

Though the NUM was opposed to this rundown, industrial action as a means of resistance to it was never on the agenda. In an era of full employment, displaced miners could still find jobs elsewhere. Many were pleased to have the opportunity of getting out of the pits into more salubrious sectors. Furthermore, as different regions were affected to different degrees by the closures, there was little chance at this time that any unity could have been forged on the issue, even had the rank and file membership and the leadership wished it. But the third aspect which should be recognised is that the leaders of the NUM themselves did not believe in assertive trade unionism; at least not for the purposes of maintaining the size of their industry. The question of the size and capacity of the industry was considered to be outside the ambit of trade unionism.

At this period, both left and right within the union accepted that it was management's prerogative to manage as it saw fit. Its only role, as far as pit closures were concerned, was perceived to be the alleviation of hardship. The idea that, following nationalisation, there were 'no opposing sides in the industry' continued to imbue the union's ethos. The 'political' and the 'industrial' were thus separated in the minds of trade unionists. There were boundaries which should not be transgressed, and certain decisions which must be left to politicians. Pit closures were one such issue. This dichotomy between the industrial and the political led the NUM to invest enormous faith in the Labour party. With the return of a Labour government, it was believed, all would be well; the contraction would stop. Thus NUM President Sidney Ford told the 1962 annual conference:

> Our only hope of government assistance lies in the return of a Labour government.[3]

Such a Labour government was elected in 1964; yet far from reversing the rundown in coal, Harold Wilson's administration in fact intensified the previous Tory policies and speeded up pit closures. Though Labour had, prior to the election, promised a coal industry which would be extracting 200 million tons a year, and stated in its 1964 election manifesto that 'major expansion programmes will be needed in the existing nationalised industries', Wilson's government reneged on these pledges. In fact the period of the 1964–70 Labour government saw the most dramatic and ruthless contraction of the industry in its post-war history. Between 1964 and 1968 the number of collieries in operation fell by 40 per cent, and manpower by a similar figure. Between 1965 and 1969, 200 collieries were closed. In other words, for four years one pit closed almost every week. This was the third, and most dramatic, phase of post-war pit closures.

Obviously, the vast majority of these collieries were by no means physically exhausted of coal deposits. They were closed, quite simply, because the Labour government took a conscious, political decision to adhere to international free-market considerations as regards national energy policy. The price of oil continued to fall, in relative terms, *vis-à-vis* that of coal. The advent of giant oil tankers and brand new refineries meant that oil was cheap and plentiful, and coal could not hope to match it. Multinational oil companies could also offer special discounts to break into a particular market, or cross-subsidise by using a higher price charged to some customers to cover a lower price charged to others. The NCB, by contrast, was debarred from adopting similar tactics by statute.

The NUM's response to this rapid contraction was once again one of acquiescence and co-operation. Full employment meant that, at least for the young and fit, there were jobs to be had elsewhere. On the other hand, for the older men, even then, there was very little else, and the remaining workforce was influenced both by its advancing average age and the fact that the coal industry was increasingly being seen as obsolete. Mobilising such a workforce into taking industrial action to save pits would have been a task of Sisyphean proportions. A second factor militating against resistance during this phase was the miners' loyalty to Labour and the fear that disruption might precipitate the return of a Tory government which, it was felt, would be worse.

But the third factor influencing the lack of resistance was that the NUM's leadership had, in any case, accepted much of the logic of the case for deindustrialisation. Sidney Ford shared the Labour leadership's vision of a smaller, more compact, competitive coal industry. Ford summed up his view thus:

If we are to obtain the reforms and improvements to which we believe our members are entitled, the industry will have to sell its product, and this will have to be done in the face of keen competition especially from oil.[4]

However, at this time, a minority faction began to develop within the union. Its object was to mobilise industrial muscle to halt the contraction. The Derbyshire Area, for example, published a pamphlet in 1964 entitled *A Plan for the Miners*, which argued for resistance to pit closures. And a rank-and-file delegate from Woolley Colliery, near Barnsley, called Arthur Scargill, told the 1967 annual conference what his view was of Power Minister Richard Marsh's speech the day before.

I can honestly say that I never heard flannel like we got from the Minister. . .He said we have got nuclear power stations with us, whether we like it or not. I suggest to this Conference that we have got coal mines with us. . .but they did something about this problem: they closed them down. This was a complete reversal of the policy. . .that was promised by the Labour government before it was put into office. . .This represents a betrayal of the mining industry.[5]

The major problem faced by those who wished to fight pit closures was that the NUM had been permeated by the logic of free-market ideas; and, at least at national level, by the tendency, since nationalisation, towards co-operation with management. Their main political task was to create a 'counter-hegemony' within the union. This would seek to break the ideological bond between, on the one hand, those who advocated adherence to capitalist logic—successive governments, union leaders such as Sidney Ford and the NCB—and, on the other, the NUM itself. This 'counter-hegemony' would be constructed by the only available means: leafleting, holding public meetings, taking the initiative at grassroots level in advocating industrial action by workers, and offering leadership for such action. The proponents of the 'counter-hegemony' also understood clearly that it was vital to their campaign to win the leadership of one of the large coalfield areas. That would strengthen their position immensely, and from that established base, progress could be made towards developing the political consciousness of the miners nationwide.

Meanwhile the Labour government left office in 1970, and were replaced by the Conservatives under the leadership of Edward Heath. The 1970s represents the fourth post-war phase in the politics of the size of the coal industry. The massive pit closure programme itself had tailed off—indeed so many pits had been closed under the previous Labour government that the 'high cost' end of the industry had largely been eliminated. And in the early

1970s there were clear signs of an oil crisis on the horizon. Yet the practice of closing 'uneconomic' pits, on a much reduced scale because fewer pits were regarded as such, was continued. Each year under the Heath government pits were closed on these grounds. Nor was this process to cease with the advent of the 1974–9 Labour government. Despite the major oil crises of the 1970s, which had resulted in renewed optimism for the domestic coal industry, and despite the tripartite agreement in 1974 on expansion in the coal industry, called 'Plan for Coal', pits continued to be closed during this period because they were uneconomic. Rockingham Colliery, near Barnsley, was closed for this reason in 1977, for example, as was Teversal, on the Nottinghamshire-Derbyshire border in 1978. In the five years up to April 1980, the union accepted the closure of 27 collieries, involving the loss of 14,000 jobs.

Pit closures in this fourth phase were carried out on an occasional and periodic basis by both Tory and Labour administrations, but in the overall context of an industry maintaining or expanding output. The Colliery Review Procedure, the joint consultation mechanism set up in 1973 by the Heath government in response to the world energy crisis, was the agency through which such closures were processed. Through it, the NUM could object to proposals concerning particular pits. On most occasions, however, such objections merely resulted in the delay of the closure.

These underlying trends of the early 1970s were in any case overwhelmed by the miners' pay strikes in 1972 and 1974. In a very real sense, those strikes were the legacy of successive governments' attitudes towards coal. The massive programme of pit closures, and progressively declining real wages, had left miners not only demoralised but also bitter. Relieved of the 'loyalty' constraint posed by the existence of a Labour government, miners were now more open to suggestions that trade union assertiveness could and should be employed to improve their relative position within society.

Although the 1974 strike had the more spectacular political results, it was the one of 1972 which had the most profound effects on relations between government and miners. In the context of this discussion, the important dimensions of the strike were twofold. First, the self-confidence of the miners and their union, following years of passivity, was restored. Following the Wilberforce Committee of Inquiry, the miners were to receive almost everything they had asked for. The NUM were the clear victors in the battle. Secondly, as a protagonist in the organisation and mobilisation of 'flying pickets', the 1972 strike was to give Arthur Scargill, who still did not hold an official position within the union, his first public platform. The building of the 'counter-hegemony' developed in earnest after the miners' victory of 1972. From that moment onwards, the left, with its espousal of trade union assertiveness and industrial action, was in the ascendancy. Scargill himself, following and largely as a result of, the 1972 strike, was elected first as Area Compensation Agent in Yorkshire and, later, in May 1973, Yorkshire Area President by an overwhelming majority.

The election of the Thatcher Government in 1979 ushered in the fifth phase of pit closures and heralded the longest national strike in a basic industry in British history. The rise of the radical right in the Conservative party, and subsequently in the Government, had been matched in the NUM by the rise of the radical left. Arthur Scargill had been elected National President with an unprecedently large majority in December 1981. For the first time in its history, the union had a left-wing president—a president, moreover, who was strongly committed to the advocacy of industrial action where and when necessary to stop uneconomic pits being closed. The 'counter-hegemony' had at last reached the highest office in the Union. The Government, for its part, had come to power emphasising the need to promote the primacy of free-market forces, and the need to cut back trade union strength. In such circumstances, it became inevitable that, sooner or later, there would be a clash between the NUM and the Government.

The clash came in February 1981, when, following the general recession in the economy, Derek Ezra, Chairman of the NCB declared that the coal industry was extracting seven million tons a year surplus coal. Pits would have to close. Overall, it was proposed that 23 pits should close during the financial year 1981–2. The union's response to this closure programme was swift and erupted spontaneously, especially in the coalfields most threatened. Following widespread unofficial grassroots action and the threat of an all-out national strike, the Government's capitulation, when it came on 18 February 1981, was dramatic. The NCB withdrew its closure programme after the Government had agreed to relax financial constraints. It was a humiliation for Mrs Thatcher's administration, though Arthur Scargill himself believed that talk of a total victory by the miners was premature, and that the Government had merely postponed the date of battle.

Scargill was to be proved right. Re-elected in 1983 with an overwhelming majority in the House of Commons, the Thatcher government felt confident enough to push ahead with earlier plans. Ian MacGregor, formerly of British Steel and now Mrs Thatcher's personal appointee in September 1983 to the chairmanship of the NCB, told the NUM on 6 March 1984 that deep-mined capacity was to be cut in the financial year 1984–5 by 4 million tons, which it was calculated would mean the loss of 21,000 jobs.

MacGregor made it clear that his wider aim was to prune the industry to 'market clearing levels' which, given the economic situation of the NCB was likely to mean a much more draconian run-down.

The most significant factor in the 1984–5 miners' strike that followed was not the substantial minority of workers who continued to work throughout the dispute, nor the number of men who drifted back to work, but the fact that a strike over pit closures could have been pursued on a national basis at all. Pit closures are, as noted earlier, a divisive phenomenon: not all miners, or all coalfields, are affected by them to the same extent. Prior to the 1980s, such a strike would not have been possible. An attempt to implant an overtime ban in 1976 over the impending closure of the 'uneconomic' Langwith colliery in Derbyshire, for example, had failed to get off the ground. The fact that a line of resistance could be adopted by the miners in the 1980s owes a great deal to the development of the 'counter-hegemony' within the union itself. This was partly due to the work of individuals within the union, and partly due to the influence of external social and economic changes—chiefly, the re-emergence of mass unemployment, which had hit many coalfield areas particularly severely. The decision to contract the coal industry in the 1980s because of falling demand can be compared, and contrasted, with the implementation of contraction in the same industry two decades earlier. As was noted, the 1960s saw very little opposition to a much more severe run-down.

In effect, the 1984–5 miners' strike turned into a conflict wider than a dispute solely over pit closures. It developed into a symbolic war between those who insisted that there was no alternative to the pursuance of a social market strategy in industrial and economic policy; and those ranged against them who believed that an alternative to the mass unemployment of the early and mid-1980s must be possible.

At the heart of the conflict between the miners and the NCB, backed by the Government, was the dispute over what constituted an uneconomic pit; and, even where pits could be deemed uneconomic, whether or not they should be closed. And there is a further corollary: in what circumstances should a pit be closed if not in accordance with the market? How is provision made for a 'positive adjustment' in the economy, the orderly and progressive contraction of sectors whose products are in declining demand, or whose technology is superseded by another? How is provision to be made for the reallocation of capital and labour to industrial sectors which are ripe for expansion, and/or where there may be opportunities for new jobs?

Right-wing economists Patrick Minford and Peter Kunk, for example, argued in November 1984 that the closure of all Britain's 'uneconomic' pits would have resulted in a net creation of 50,000 jobs at a national level. This would occur 'naturally' as labour was freed from this 'unproductive' sector and subsidies from the public purse to the coal industry were reduced, contributing towards a position where taxes could be cut. Minford, who has been one of Mrs Thatcher's chief advisers on economics, and is a professor at Liverpool University, even went as far as to suggest in November 1984 that the 1984–5 miners' strike was a good thing for the British economy.

It does not appear to have occurred to many people that if these pits do not produce it will be a good thing. . .They are predominantly high cost; the longer they stay shut, the less their prospects of reopening.[6]

Defenders of the NUM's position would argue that this type of analysis loses its cogency if it is probed for what it leaves out of the analysis; and makes the mistake of treating coal as if it were exactly the same as any other commodity traded in the capitalist market, amenable to the same ineluctable economic 'laws'. Their contention would be that there are special factors relating to the coal industry, factors which cannot be ignored when the decision is being taken as to whether or not to keep open an 'uneconomic' pit, and factors which must sometimes override the signals from the market place.

First of all, they would argue, it should be recognised that the decision to close a pit is an irreversible one. Those taking that decision should be aware that they are engaging in the permanent sterilisation of what is sometimes millions of tons of coal. Unlike other industries, production units in the coal industry cannot be opened and closed, established and disestablished, in order to meet cyclical variations in demand. In the manufacture of bicycles, for example, if there is a fall in demand one year, the bicycle factory can be closed in order to balance supply with demand. If, however, demand picks up the following year, it does not present overwhelming difficulties to reopen the original factory, or construct a new one somewhere, in order to meet the increased demand. Such options are not available in the coal industry. A new pit takes between eight and ten years to sink and come into full production. Who can predict what demand for coal will be in a decade's time? For these reasons, a decision to close a pit which still holds reserves of coal, but which is deemed uneconomic to mine, should not be taken lightly, or solely with regard to market forces.

E.F. Schumacher, economic adviser to the NCB from 1950 to 1970, expressed the matter thus:

To close a pit is an irreversible decision. Once a pit is closed it is not possible to reopen it except by the expenditure of a vast amount of capital. To keep a pit on a care and maintenance basis is so expensive that, in fact, it is never done. So these irreversible decisions have to be taken and they have to make sense, not just now, but also twenty, thirty or forty years hence.[7]

Connected with these arguments is the contention that coal, as a non-renewable, finite commodity, is not directly equivalent to most other commodities traded in the capitalist market. According to Schumacher, traded commodities fit into two categories, primary and secondary.

Let no one think that the economic importance of £3 worth of coal is the same as that of £3 worth of any other commodity. There are only two basic items in the world economy—food and fuel. All the rest are secondary.[8]

Thus pits which have been closed on the grounds that they were uneconomic to mine were closed because, mistakenly, fuel was regarded as being a 'secondary' commodity.

Additionally, the justification of pit closures on market criteria ignores the costs to future generations of pursuing such a policy. Again, Schumacher has summed up this argument well.

When applied to renewable goods such terms as 'cost of production', 'depreciation', 'economic or uneconomic' have a fairly clear meaning. For instance, it is uneconomic to cultivate area 'A' if better results could be obtained by cultivating area 'B' instead and if only one of the two areas is needed to meet demand. Is the same true when 'A' represents coal deposits, that is, non-renewable resources? Coal 'B' may indeed be cheaper to get than coal 'A' but it can only be got once. When it is gone, coal 'A' must be resorted to, whether we like it or not. In other words, we are not choosing to use 'B' *instead* of 'A', but merely to take 'B' *before* taking 'A'. This is not an economic choice at all. 'Best seams first' is not a principle of economics. (What to take now and what to leave for later is, in fact, a question of ethics, not of economics.) The master of the wedding feast who gives the best wine first and leaves the poor wines for later cannot invoke the principles of economics for his actions, and he who leaves the best wines for the end cannot be accused of acting uneconomically.[9]

Crucial to an understanding of the politics of 'uneconomic' pits is also an examination of the pricing policy of the agency selling the coal, in this case the NCB. David Thomas has recounted, for example, how the Thatcher government kept down prices of coal going to power stations, but allowed the price of electricity to rise by increments well above the rate of inflation.[10] Since about four-fifths of fuel normally used at power stations is coal, the electricity industry was been helped to profitability, while the NCB suffered opprobrium as a result of continuing losses. It is in this context, so the argument runs, that pits were declared uneconomic by the NCB under the aegis of the Government.

Furthermore, the accountancy techniques employed by the NCB in the 1980s have been challenged from various sources. An article published in January 1985 in *Accountancy*, the journal of the Institute of Chartered Accountants, for example, written by David Cooper, the Price Waterhouse Professor of Accounting and Finance at the University of Manchester Institute of Science and Technology (UMIST), and Tony Lowe, Professor of Accountancy and Financial Management at the University of Sheffield, argued that the NCB's internal accounting procedures 'fail to form an adequate basis for informed management decisions.'

A major conclusion of the report was that the NCB should take into consideration the fact that a large proportion of an individual colliery's costs are fixed or central overheads, costs which will not be saved if a pit is closed but which will have to be reallocated to pits continuing in operation. The fact that a smaller number of pits would be open after a programme of pit closures would mean higher fixed costs at each of them.[11] Mrs Thatcher herself was not impressed by the arguments of this report. She informed the House of Commons of its implications:

> If you regard the whole matter of coal as merely accounting and think it can all be done with mirrors, then you will be quite happy if we eliminate the £1.3 billion subsidy a year. That is not a matter of accounting. That is a matter of fact.[12]

Another report published in December 1984 by Dr Bill Robinson of the London Business School, which is usually sympathetic to the Thatcher position, was also critical of the NCB's accountancy practices. Robinson's report argued that a maximum of 20,000 pit jobs might have to be shed if the NCB was to return to economic viability.[13] Now while this figure did equate roughly with the NCB's reductions in labour for 1984–5, it was a long way short of the figure implied by the NCB's and the Government's own break-even targets, and the reduction of manpower that actually occurred.

Andrew Glyn also launched attacks throughout 1984 on the theoretical basis of the NCB's and the Government's analysis of the financial position of the coal industry. His basic thesis was that many of the costs facing the coal industry in the 1980s were a legacy of past mining operations, and should not necessarily be counted as part of the cost of coal-mining in 1984. Thus, of the NCB's £1.3 billion financial loss for 1983–4, £358 million was accounted for by 'operating losses'; £467 million went to interest payments; £344 million financed 'social costs' and an additional £150 million was direct government payments to redundant mineworkers. The biggest part of the £358 million 'operating losses', in fact £245 million, was taken up by repairing 'surface damage', in other words, subsidence.

1983–4 had seen a rush of subsidence problems, particularly around Mansfield. As Glyn pointed out, this was not a reflection of current costs of mining, however, but a legacy of past coal-mining operations. Even if pits closed, such costs would still have to be met. A further item covered under the title 'charges in respect of past employees' came to £130 million in 1983–4. In fact this referred mainly to pensions to past employees. As Glyn pointed out, this cannot be regarded as a cost attributable to current mining operations. Again it is a legacy of past mining. Such claims for pensions and subsidence would have to be met even if the whole NCB operation closed down. The £245 million and £130 million together more than account for the NCB's operating losses for 1983–4; if they are left out the NCB made an operating profit over that financial year. There is no particular reason for such costs to be borne by those who use coal, via higher prices, or by those who mine coal, via lower wages. It does not constitute a subsidy of current coal production if they are met by the taxpayer. Nor do 'social costs' of £344 million subsidise the cost of mining coal in the 1980s: they are, in fact, the costs of not producing coal because they cover mainly 'costs in respect of the closure of uneconomic capacity or redundancy of employees'. The same argument applies to the direct government grants to redundant mineworkers: such costs of maintaining unemployed workers, indeed, contribute to the arguments against the closure of collieries in the first place. On the final item in the £1.3 billion deficit, the interest payments, Glyn had this to say:

> The final item which has to be 'subsidised' by the Government is the £467m of interest payments (£400m of which go straight back to the Government). This huge figure directly reflects both the high interest rate policy of the Government and the fact that so much of the NCB's investment has been financed by fixed interest loans.
>
> It actually represents a return of 6.3 per cent on the (replacement) value of the capital employed. This is about double the corresponding rate of profit in private manufacturing industry in recent years. So this part of the 'subsidy' is mainly paid by the Government to itself to give itself an inflated rate of profit.[14]

Glyn's assertions were supported to some extent by a further report published in September 1984 from Gavyn Davies of the

City stockbrokers Simon and Coates and Professor David Metcalfe of the University of Kent. Their report suggested that it was insufficient to use NCB finance and accounting conventions to define 'uneconomic' pits, because within such conventions accommodation was not made for social costs resulting from closures or the true value of providing jobs for people in an underemployed economy such as Britain's in the 1980s.[15]

It should also be recognised that profitability is often investment-led. Pits that have been starved of investment will tend to become 'uneconomic'. A major contention of the miners during the 1984–5 dispute was that throughout the Thatcher years the overwhelming majority of investment in the coal industry had been directed to the Selby 'superpit' project, to the detriment of other pits and coalfields.

In addition, the price of British coal in relation to foreign coal and alternative forms of energy, and hence its domestic and international competitiveness, can be affected significantly by changes in the exchange rate of sterling and in the costs of international freighting. A high exchange rate would make British coal more expensive *vis-à-vis* foreign coal. Through the Thatcher years the external value of sterling has been volatile, but in general the Government seems to have been quite happy with a high exchange rate and even appears to have been aiming for one.

What emerges from this analysis, therefore, is that even if a policy of closing uneconomic pits can be agreed, there are enormous difficulties in defining what that term means.

The effect of the 1984–5 miners' strike was effectively to break the power of the NUM, the union most often considered to be in the vanguard of the Labour movement. It did so because it allowed for a dramatic diminution in its membership, provided for the rise of the breakaway Union of Democratic Mineworkers (UDM), the nucleus of which was the rebel Nottinghamshire mineworkers, who, for the most part, refused to join the strike, in Nottinghamshire, Leicestershire and Warwickshire, and moreover, because it was a resounding defeat for Arthur Scargill and the NUM.

The Government believes that all industry should be in the private sector, and despite its special status as the 'jewel in the crown' of nationalisation, coal can be no exception. If the Conservatives stay in power in the 1990s, then it is certain that British Coal will be privatised in the early part of the decade. In retrospect, one can argue that the management of the coal industry spent the whole of the 1980s preparing for privatisation. Several things has to be done before it could become attractive to private buyers. First, the power of Arthur Scargill and the NUM had to be broken. That was effected with the defeat of the NUM in the strike and the rise of the UDM. Secondly, flexible working had to be introduced instead of the standard five-day week stubbornly defended by Scargill and the NUM. This would mean pits could be worked for longer—300 days a year instead of 233—and that expensive machinery could be used more efficiently; the overall effect would be that coal would be mined more cheaply. British Coal announced in August 1988 that a flexible working agreement, based around a six-day working week, had been successfully negotiated with the UDM for new pits and pits where large investments were being made. Later, sole negotiating rights in such pits were given to the UDM.

Thirdly, of course, there was a need to move into profitability, and the chosen strategy for this—probably the only strategy available—was to close down 'uneconomic' pits while at the same time concentrating production in a smaller number of 'superpits', as well as introducing flexible working. New superpits are planned at Asfordby in Leicestershire and just outside Coventry in the Warwickshire coalfield. Selby remains an important project, and the development of a superpit at Margam in South Wales is expected.

Yet despite the changes in the industry, and despite an operating profit of £216 million in 1987–8, the overall total loss, after interest payments and restructuring costs, was £540 million for that year. Operating costs had fallen, and productivity had risen dramatically during the late 1980s.

The NUM will bitterly oppose privatisation when it comes, arguing that it means a return to the bad old days when private owners jeopardised the safety of men (and, further back in history, women and children) in order to increase profits. They will point out that the mining unions had fought for public ownership of coal mines since the turn of the century. They will remind people how nationalisation in the 1940s generated enormous optimism amongst ordinary miners.

But, with their power diminished, it is unlikely that they will be able to stop the process. Advocates of privatisation will argue that the NUM's warnings against private ownership belong to the past, and that one cannot live one's life in an industrial museum. They will argue that British Coal has more chance of prospering once it is freed from state control, and that miners themselves will be better off.

The coal industry certainly has a future in Britain, but it is an uncertain one. Once the British electricity industry, generation and distribution, is privatised, that future will become less certain still as British Coal's main customer looks around the world for the cheapest source of coal. Its future is also threatened by the existence and potential growth of nuclear power as an alternative means of electricity generation, an industry to which the Thatcher governments have been heavily committed.

NOTES

1. Quoted in Hall (1981), p. 194.
2. House of Commons Official Report, Vol. 392, Column 921, 1943.
3. National Union of Mineworkers Annual Conference Report, 1962, p. 126.
4. Quoted in Hall (1981), p. 121.
5. National Union of Mineworkers Annual Conference Report, 1967, p. 249.
6. The *Financial Times*, 15 November 1984.
7. Quoted in Kirk, p. 86.
8. Quoted in Kirk, pp. 4–5.
9. Quoted in Kirk, p. 6.
10. D. Thomas: 'The Secret War Against Coal', *New Socialist*, No. 11, September 1984.
11. The *Guardian*, 28 November 1984.
12. The *Guardian*, 7 December 1984.
13. The *Guardian*, 10 December 1984.
14. A. Glyn: 'Propped Up with Prejudice', the *Guardian*, 7 August 1984.
15. The *Guardian*, 24 September 1984.

Case Study 2: The Politics of Nuclear Power

While most industries can claim to be 'politically charged' in the sense that, at some time or other, there will have been disputes between workers and owners over such things as levels of pay or conditions of work, or disputes between the industry and government over the awarding of orders or similar arguments, there are few where it is the technology itself that is in question. That is the case, however, with nuclear power or, to be more precise, the generation of electricity for civil purposes by the use of nuclear technology. For this reason, and because, in broader terms, the politics of energy industries are never far from the top of the political agenda, it is important to examine the politics of nuclear power.

The case against nuclear power can be put succinctly. First, if there is a major accident at a nuclear power station, then its consequences are likely to be devastating. Radioactive fall-out from such an accident can travel thousands of miles, contaminating food, animals, water and land in distant continents. Thousands of acres of agricultural and other land may be contaminated for thousands of years into the future. Unborn generations may be affected as damaged genes are inherited. And, as the effects of radioactive fall-out can take time to manifest themselves, no one can be quite sure of the full extent of the damage caused by an accident: there may be people still contracting cancer twenty years after the event. Secondly, the waste generated by the production of electricity by nuclear means remains 'hot' in radioactive terms, and therefore dangerous, for thousands of years. Critics argue there is no safe way of storing this waste, or decontaminating it, and that therefore stocks of it will continue to mount up. Opponents of nuclear power also point a finger at clusters of leukemia at higher than average rates around nuclear power stations and reprocessing plants.

A fourth argument they level against the civil power industry is that, under its guise, the more sinister production of nuclear weapons is taking place. Because plutonium, the raw material for the production of nuclear weapons, can be extracted from the waste left from nuclear electricity generation, the former Labour cabinet minister and prominent Labour left-winger Tony Benn has claimed that every nuclear power station in Britain is a potential bomb factory. Others on the left have argued that nuclear power is simply a means of reducing the power of the miners' trade unions. Indeed, Cecil Parkinson, the Secretary of State for Energy, defended the Government's decision to enforce privatised distribution companies to buy 20 per cent of their electricity from nuclear-generated sources by saying in August 1988:

> Without the nuclear programme during the miners' strike, even with the use of oil, it's quite possible that as a country we would not have been able to survive, and that Mr. Scargill could have his way.[1]

By the late 1980s, nuclear power stations were capable of supplying 20 per cent of Britain's electricity; if Scotland is looked at separately, however, the figure is higher, up to 40 per cent.

In addition to these political and environmental arguments against nuclear power, there are also those who say it has been an abject *industrial* failure in Britain. The first nuclear power stations in Britain were called Magnox reactors; the British design which superseded them was the Advanced Gas-Cooled Reactor (AGR). The AGR was to be at the forefront of Britain's great technological revolution; it would provide export orders for British industry; it would provide cheap electricity; it would be safe and cheap to build. In practice, it failed to gain a single export order. The cost of building them and the time it took were phenomenal. As Tony Hall notes:

> Work on the Dungeness B (AGR) power station began in 1966. It was not finished until nearly two decades later. The cost in real terms was over twice the original estimate. Dungeness B became synonymous with the failure of Britain's nuclear industry.[2]

Industrialists have often argued that one of the reasons they have had difficulty in competing with foreign manufacturers is that energy costs have been higher in Britain than abroad. But the AGR failed in this respect also, along with the rest of Britain's nuclear power stations. A table produced in 1982 by the Central Electricity Generating Board (CEGB) showed coal to be the fuel which generated the cheapest electricity:

Generating Costs—pence per kilowatt-hour

Major Stations Commissioned between 1965 and 1977			Most Recently Commissioned Nuclear and Coal Stations	
Magnox (Nuclear)	Coal	Oil	Hinkley Point B (Nuclear)	Drax (first half) (coal)
2.60	2.19	2.49	2.92	2.30[3]

The CEGB admitted in December 1988 that the nuclear power stations it planned to build after privatisation could be far more expensive than alternative coal-fired plants.[4] The final humiliation for the British-designed AGR came when the Government announced in 1987 that it would be the American-designed Pressurised Water Reactor (PWR) that would form the basis of the next generation of nuclear plants, with the first one being built at Sizewell in Suffolk. There would be no more AGRs.

Proponents of nuclear power respond by arguing that these opponents are merely latter-day Luddities, against anything which is modern and scientifically advanced. As for the waste, they point out:

A significant factor about nuclear waste is the relatively small amount produced. If all the electricity one individual uses in his life-time were generated by coal-fired power stations 30 tonnes of ash would be produced. If it were generated by nuclear power less than a kilogramme of highly active waste and a few kilogrammes of fuel cladding would be produced. . . The concentrated liquid waste from the entire British nuclear programme over the last quarter of a century is equivalent in volume to two three-bedroomed houses.[5]

Nuclear power will be necessary, they argue, when the oil runs out, which may be sooner than 2050, and when coal is required for other purposes, such as conversion into gas and petrol. The radiation people receive from nuclear power stations and reproducing plants is less than they receive from natural background radiation. Moreover, they contrast the safety record of Britain's nuclear power industry with that of its coal industry. In the latter, as everybody knows, thousands have been killed and injured over the years. In the former, so its proponents claim, no one has been killed.

That in itself is a claim which is open to some dispute. The nuclear industry in Britain has, on several occasions, made out-of-court compensation settlements, without conceding liability, to the families of people who have died after working in the industry. Further, anti-nuclear campaigners claim that to make comparisons between a coal mine and a nuclear power station is not to compare like with like; instead, they say, the *whole cycle* of electricity production, from the mining of uranium through to reprocessing, should be compared. In this connection, a brochure published by the Anti-Nuclear Campaign in the early 1980s said:

> out of 100 uranium miners being monitored from one uranium mine in New Mexico, USA, 25 have already died of cancer while still in their forties; and a further 20 are suffering from cancer.

and

> The incidence of leukemia/cancer among white Australian uranium miners has been found to be six times the expected norm; and three times the expected norm was found among mill workers.[6]

The opponents' trump card is the argument that nuclear power stations are, essentially, just machines, and like any other machine, they can go wrong. Even if the machine itself does not go wrong, then the humans who operate it might make mistakes. Humans are fallible. And, if they do make a series of mistakes, the consequences for the world are disastrous. As if any confirmation were needed, the nuclear disaster, the world's worst, at Chernobyl in the USSR in 1986, proved that beyond any doubt.

This disaster proved to be a catalyst for political opposition to nuclear power in Europe and further afield. In Britain, opposition intensified for a while before reverting to its normal form: muted, represented by a host of disparate and sometimes competing pressure groups, and with no clear focus. As a political issue nuclear energy has always had a fairly low profile in Britain. And, until Chernobyl, most of the muted disquiet surrounding nuclear energy had been focused on nuclear leaks from the reprocessing plant at Sellafield, and was primarily concerned with ensuring adequate safety standards and a minimum of pollution, rather than manifesting itself as opposition to the nuclear industry as a form of technology. Yet this is in contrast to the situations in two of Britain's most comparable neighbours, West Germany and France. In West Germany, opposition to the industry is long-standing and has often taken aggressive forms. In France, while there is a fairly strong political consensus underpinning the nuclear industry, what opposition there has been has often been of a violent nature.

Plans to go ahead with nuclear programmes have initiated political responses which have varied in intensity in the different countries. Nevertheless, all three have seen opposition in some form. This has been directed against proposed reactor sites; against the dumping of nuclear waste, on land or at sea; and against reprocessing plants and facilities. The most intense and widespread opposition was seen in West Germany in the 1970s and 1980s. It was largely the issue of nuclear power, alongside nuclear weapons, which was the catalyst in the rise of the Greens. Nuclear power proposals have also been fought in the courts—in other words by utilising the legal system rather than the political—and this has caused considerable delays to certain programmes. In addition, there have been widespread and well-reported confrontations between demonstrators and the police, at which the latter have not been slow to employ strong-arm tactics to quell disturbances. The late 1980s saw violent demonstrations at Wackersdorf in Bavaria, the construction site for West Germany's first nuclear fuel reprocessing plant. It witnessed occupations and mass demonstrations. In January 1986 there was a confrontation between demonstrators and the police in which the authorities moved in with chain saws and mobile cranes to tear down huts erected by the demonstrating occupants. Revealingly, the West German authorites have sought to calm opposition to Wackersdorf by assurances that 'a Sellafield could not happen here'. Since Chernobyl, the opposition Social Democratic Party (SPD) has come out against the construction of the Wackersdorf plant. So, while Chernobyl has heightened and intensified opposition to nuclear power in West Germany, that opposition has a long history. Earlier demonstrations frequently involved as many as 100,000 people.

While at a party political level nuclear energy in France has enjoyed the security of a pro-nuclear consensus, there has nevertheless been some notable grassroots opposition to nuclear power over the same period, with demonstrators often adopting militant, confrontational strategies. For example, in July 1977, opposition to the construction of the fast breeder reactor at Super-Phenix at Malville led to an attempted occupation of the site by 60,000 people. A battle ensued lasting three hours, with riot police using batons and tear gas to fight back the tens of thousands of demonstrators. There were other very large battles of this sort, particularly at Plogoff in Brittany which had been chosen as the site for a 'nuclear park' of four reactors. In March 1980 there were widespread protests there culminating in the largest demonstration ever seen in France. Plogoff was also an example of protest having the desired effect. It was one of the few nuclear projects to be cancelled by President François Mitterand's new Socialist government soon after assuming office in May 1981.

In Britain several events could have acted as potential catalysts of public opposition, mainly problems encountered by British Nuclear Fuels at Windscale/Sellafield in the 1970s and, more particularly, the 1980s. There were several worrying discharges and leaks (the difference depending on whether they were intended or not), culminating in the successful prosecution of the company in the 1980s. The 1984–5 miners' strike provided a potential opportunity for those interested to focus on the fact that in the 1980s and 1990s Britain faces a choice between coal or nuclear energy, or some combination of both. As it was, the issue was largely overlooked as protagonists became embroiled in other areas of the dispute. The lack of opposition to nuclear power was also surprising given that in general the British population was becoming more and more interested in environmental issues. *Social Trends*, for instance, shows that Friends of the Earth increased its membership 27-fold over the period 1971–85, and the National Trust saw its membership quadruple from 315,000 to 1,300,000 over the same period. Furthermore, there have been considerable difficulties in localities earmarked for the inland dumping of nuclear waste. Prominent Tories made public their opposition to the dumping of waste in their constituencies. An opinion poll in October 1985 showed that 68 per cent of people questioned were opposed to keeping any nuclear waste at all on the British mainland. And yet, despite all these factors, there was a failure to translate these sometimes latent, sometimes localised and peripheral concerns and opposition into a political issue figuring with any importance on the political agenda.

What, then, provides the explanation for the differing responses in the different countries? The reasons fall into two categories: first, the different strategies that have been adopted in relation to nuclear power by the respective governments; secondly the differing cultural and political traditions.

The most obvious contrast between the British government on the one hand, and the French and West Germans on the other, has been the attitudes they have adopted. The French and West German governments have adopted far more aggressive postures. Take for example, the siting policies. Most of the sites for British reactors were chosen in the 1940s and 1950s, when there was considerable optimism surrounding nuclear power. Those were the days when the public was told that because of nuclear power, electricity in the future would be 'too cheap to meter'. When the reactors were built they were either tacked on to existing sites, where the local community had had time to get used to the nuclear industry, or placed in very remote locations. This served to minimise opposition, and was in marked contrast to the choosing of greenfield sites by the French and West German authorities. Recent siting policy in Britain still exhibits the phenomenon described above. An example was the choice of Dounreay as the place for a planned nuclear reprocessing plant. Dounreay has for years had an experimental nuclear fast breeder reactor, as well as being just about as remote as one can possibly get in Britain. Another aspect of the low-profile technique has been to choose sites where a hostile response from local authorities is not expected. The choosing of Tory Sizewell for the site of the first PWR is a case in point, as it already has a nuclear plant of the AGR variety.

The momentary exception to this low-profile approach was when the ill-fated Energy Secretary David Howell announced at the beginning of Mrs Thatcher's first term that one new nuclear power station would be ordered every year for the next decade. This was the catalyst for the formation of the Anti-Nuclear Campaign in 1980: a broad-based group comprised of individuals and organisations seeking an end to nuclear power in Britain. Labour and Liberal party activists joined; there was a contingent of Communist and Socialist Worker Party representation; there was a trade union presence with branches of the TGWU and NUPE joining, as well as the Austin Joint Shop Stewards at Longbridge, the NUM and a whole host of regional ecological and anti-nuclear groups. It was the classic British umbrella protest group. But it soon fizzled out, partly because the decision to go for ten reactors based on the American PWR design was quietly dropped (the decision on Sizewell, proposed as the first of these, was not taken until 1987) but mainly because it was eclipsed by the Campaign for Nuclear Disarmament (CND). Cruise missiles and the deterioration in East–West relations meant that nuclear bombs became an issue whilst nuclear power did not.

Even Howell's seeming departure from the low-profile approach was not complete. The now famous leaked cabinet minutes of 1979, referring to a meeting before Howell's announcement but related to it, which in another part lauded the merits of nuclear energy as a means of removing power from the miners' and transport workers' unions, also stressed:

> Opposition to nuclear power might well provide a focus for protest groups over the next decade, and the Government might make rapid progress towards its objective by a low profile approach, which avoided putting the Government into a position of confrontation with the protesters.[7]

Another example of a low-profile strategy was the Government's decision to abandon plans to announce inland sites for intermediate nuclear waste dumping before the general election of 1987, and its dithering over where to dump the low-level waste on land. Or one might cite the surrender to the National Union of Seamen over the latter's ban on dumping nuclear waste at sea. It would presumably have been possible, for example, to use the Royal Navy to carry out sea dumpings, but it was never done.

What encouraged the 'low profile' strategy in Britain, of course, was the fact that even following the 1973 energy crisis, vast coal reserves, the still developing oil industry and the reserves of natural gas meant that there was simply not the need in Britain to go for a crash programme of nuclear power.

All this contrasts with the situations, and the government strategies, in France and West Germany. Both countries appeared to be more determined, whatever political party was in power, to go ahead with nuclear projects. This was especially the case in France. Both countries, but again especially France, had fewer indigenous sources of energy such as coal or oil. Furthermore, there was the existence within both countries of well-organised and internationally successful nuclear industries. This contrasted with Britain, where the nuclear establishment had had to live with the debilitating effects of a conflict over choice of reactor design. There were two camps—those who supported the British AGR and those who favoured the American-designed PWR. For a period between 1974 and 1976 the situation was further complicated by a decision to go for the Steam Generating Heavy Water Reactors (SGHWR), also British designed, which was subsequently abandoned. That conflict was still raging in the late 1980s, with the South of Scotland Electricity Board (SSEB) arguing at the Sizewell Inquiry that the problems in building and operating the AGR had been overcome and that the AGR was still the best option. The CEGB and the Government wanted, and got, the PWR. The legacy of the AGR, with its construction delays, financial overruns and failure to win export orders had, however, had a debilitating effect on the British nuclear industry.

The West Germans were relatively late in getting into the nuclear field, and that itself had important political repercussions. Because of differences in the political context, the development of nuclear technology in West Germany proceeded in a different way from France and Britain. At the outset, there was not the same opportunity for the West German state to become involved in nuclear technology development, even if it had wanted to. It would have been impossible for the post-Nazi political system to have devised a national nuclear policy based on coherent nationalist ideology, as the French had done in relation to their nuclear technology development. So in sharp contrast to the

British and French experience, the West German nuclear industry began largely with private and local initiatives. As the Allied ban on nuclear research was gradually lifted, industrial participants in this field gathered momentum, but private firms waited until after the Paris Accords of 1954, which lifted all restrictions in return for Germany's pledge not to develop nuclear weapons, before setting out in earnest to explore the industrial potential of nuclear energy. And it was not until 1967 that the German Atomic Commission announced the first official nuclear plan with a programme of development.

This late entry allowed time for fears to build up in the late 1960s and 1970s about the safety aspects of nuclear energy, the perceived connection with nuclear weapons and the problems that it was feared an expanding nuclear industry would pose for civil liberties. The development of nuclear power in West Germany was taking place at the very same time that issues such as the environment and individual and civil liberties were coming to the fore. Because of this later entry, West Germany did not have the opportunity to share in the early phase of optimism about nuclear energy that had been felt in Britain and France. In France optimism manifested itself in the 1950s in the argument that the harnessing of atomic energy was crucial to the restoration of the country's former greatness. And in Britain there was a general feeling at that time that we should be proud to be still up there with the great powers at the very forefront of technological research.

Differing political and cultural traditions in the different countries have had a bearing on the type and intensity of protest that has occurred. In Britain, of course, there is a longstanding tradition of referring certain policy-making decisions to what are often extensive public inquiries. In terms of nuclear politics, the most obvious examples are the inquiry into the expansion at Windscale (later renamed Sellafield), which commenced in June 1977 and reported in March 1978; the Sizewell inquiry into whether to build a PWR there, which commenced in 1981 and did not report until 1987; and the more 'restricted' inquiry into the proposal to build a nuclear fuel reprocessing plant in Dounreay to service European fast-breeders, which took place in the late 1980s and which was circumscribed so that it looked only at things such as planning matters, rather than the substantive issues.

It could be argued that the British public inquiry system has promoted certain political effects. First it has helped to depoliticise the issue by providing a forum within which opposition groups perceive they will get a fair hearing. The fact that the inquiries have been presided over by the judiciary, with its image of political neutrality and impartiality, has reinforced this perception. Secondly, the public inquiry system in Britain has tended to militate against the growth and electoral appeal of a political party committed to 'green' values. This is illustrated by a comparison with West Germany. The latter has seen a rapid growth in Green Party popularity and parliamentary representation, while in Britain the Ecology Party (renamed Green Party) has achieved only a very small vote. While there were, of course, other reasons for the failure of the British Greens—such as the electoral system and the class-based nature of British politics—it could be that one factor also impeding their development was the failure of all other environmental groups to offer support, partly because they felt they could get their grievances aired through established political channels, in particular the public inquiry system. The growth of the Greens in West Germany arose at least in part because the political system there was unable to assimilate their demands in any other way.

In France, the public inquiry system is much weaker than it is in Britain. It is generally perceived as being a political façade behind which decisions are merely rubber-stamped. In that sense, public inquiries do not provide the same kind of political 'cooling off' channel. France has also traditionally exhibited a much stronger form of extra-parliamentary protest which has often taken the form of street demonstrations and direct action against the Government or its agents. That tradition can be traced from the French Revolution through the student protests of the late 1960s, up to the actions of present-day French farmers blocking roads and dumping produce in protest against European Community decisions. And in France, of course, the confrontational assertiveness of protesters was met and overwhelmed by an even more forthright assertiveness by authorities determined to push ahead with nuclear power.

Several aspects of political culture and the political system in West Germany have helped to influence the development of anti-nuclear protest. The judiciary is quite autonomous, reflecting the decentralised character of the German political system. German courts were able to consider substantive questions about safety and technical feasibility and, because of this, they tended to assume a powerful and independent, though often contradictory, role in nuclear disputes. Many projects were delayed by the rulings of the courts, though it was rare to see total cancellation.

The most obvious conclusion that has to be drawn is that differing state strategies towards the development of nuclear power have elicited differing political responses. Additionally, the differing political systems' abilities to assimilate 'new' political developments concerning the new industry of nuclear power, coupled with different cultural traditions, have been reflected in different forms and intensities of protest.

Following Chernobyl, nothing will ever be quite the same

again. For from then on, a worldwide perception that an accident at a nuclear power station could inflict global disaster was brought into the politics of nuclear power. Even before Chernobyl, the nuclear industry had been subject to several body blows, each of which was instrumental in contributing to nuclear energy becoming a major issue on the political agenda. For example, while the nuclear power issue continues to cause ructions in the Labour party, in 1985 the party's annual conference for the first time voted for an anti-nuclear energy line. This meant Labour became the first political party of potential governmental status in the big Western European countries to adopt such a position.

The miners' strike of 1984–5 also has a bearing on nuclear power issues in a way that might not at first be obvious. For it refutes the argument advanced by apologists for nuclear energy that it would be prohibitively expensive to phase out nuclear power. It provides the political ammunition for the industry's opponents to argue with some cogency that if alternative work cannot be found for displaced nuclear power workers, then it is up to society, via the Government, to provide for some suitable remuneration arrangements for them. After all, money was quite clearly no object for the Government when it was seeking to phase out large parts of the coal-mining industry in Yorkshire, the north-east of England, Scotland, South Wales and elsewhere. Everybody knows that millions were spent in redundancy payments, in paying and transporting and billeting police up and down the country, in propaganda campaigns by the NCB, in bailing out industries such as the railways which lost most of their freight market; not to mention the millions lost by private companies and traders, or the lost taxation that would otherwise have been recouped.

With the privatisation of the electricity industry in the early 1990s, a greater question mark hangs over the future of the nuclear power industry. Quite simply the two private generating companies that will take over electricity generation in England and Wales, the two in Scotland and the one in Northern Ireland, and any other private generating companies which enter the field, will be seeking the lowest-cost electricity for the minimum capital outlay, in order to maximise profits. Although two of these companies will inherit nuclear power stations, it may be judged that future investments would be better directed elsewhere: if the world price of coal stays low, possibly in that direction.

The lifeline that has been thrown to the nuclear industry by the Thatcher government is the requirement that the new privately owned companies that are responsible for distributing electricity to consumers should obtain between 15 and 20 per cent of it from non-fossil-fuel, and therefore effectively nuclear, sources. In addition, all consumers of electricity will be required to pay a 'nuclear tax' to cover the costs of capital investment in nuclear power stations, the decommissioning of old stations, and if necessary, the higher cost of electricity generation from nuclear stations. This decision speaks volumes for the Government's energy strategy. If nuclear power was so efficient, would not private sector companies generate electricity by it, and distribution companies use it, anyway? If the real motive is to keep the power of the miners' unions in check, is this not amply provided for by simply allowing the private electricity companies, as they are to be, to import coal freely? Most importantly, the decision indicates that the Government's adherence to the principle of the free market can be overthrown if the *political* reasons are strong enough.

Opponents of nuclear power have long argued that the 'plutonium economy' would bring with it dire consequences for civil liberties, because of the opportunities it would present to terrorists and because workers at nuclear plants might have to be denied certain trade union rights. But their most incisive arguments now relate to the much wider implications posed for freedom by nuclear power. They would argue that, following Chernobyl, the freedom that is potentially threatened is the very fundamental freedom to walk in the open air, to drink the water and the milk, to eat the foods we choose without fear of contamination. In fact, their most potent argument is that the very existence of nuclear power plants has now become pyschologically depressing.

NOTES

1. The *Guardian*, 15 August 1988.
2. Hall (1986), p. 92.
3. CEGB: Analysis of Generating Costs, 1983. (Lifetime to date, 5 per cent opportunity basis.)
4. The *Independent*, 7 December 1988.
5. Nuclear Waste Management (UKAEA, London, 1981).
6. Anti-Nuclear Campaign pamphlet, *Uranium – the Plain Facts*, undated but *c*.1981.
7. Quoted in J. Valentine, *Atomic Crossroads. Before and After Sizewell* (Merlin Press, London, 1985), p. 224.

PART FIVE
Conclusion

Conclusion

Politics is really about power: who holds it, who wields it, why and for what objectives, who *should* hold it, and who is powerless. Beliefs, opinions, ideologies are important too, of course, but only if a person or group has power to pursue them and put them into effect. Without power, beliefs, ideologies and opinions are just the scabbard without the sword; empty and liable to be discarded by people and political parties. In essence, this is the battle that has occupied the Labour party for much of the 1980s: which route to power? Can power be won without sacrificing cherished beliefs?

Politics in industry is no exception to the general rule that power is a key concept to its understanding; nor does politics in industry exist in isolation from the rest of political life. Industry is one of the stages upon which politics is played out. That is why the key actors are interest groups: trade unions, business groups of one sort or another, consumer pressure groups and, more on the margins perhaps, environmental pressure groups. Interest groups exist to pursue their interests, and therefore the key question facing governments is how that should be allowed to happen. Should there be no regulation, so that the strong can suppress the weak? Should there be periodic, formalised negotiations involving the government, as in a 'corporatist' system?

Power is really at the centre of all the topics discussed here: should power reside at the level of some Euro-super state, or of national governments? Should workers have power over the running of the firms they work for? Should the rich be more powerful than the poor? Who should exercise power in the future, and in what ways? Is Britain constrained in the way it can make judgements as to who should hold power by the fact that it needs to ensure the firms in its economy remain internationally competitive?

Power is the reason why the left are so interested in—and so critical of—multinational enterprises, the City, of many of the actions of big business. To them, society is, above all else, a class-based society. Multinationals, the City, big business represent the pantheon of a ruling, exploitative class. Trade unions represent merely the untarnished defenders of an oppressed and heroic class.

Power is also the basic reason why the right in British politics is so critical of trade unions. As they see it, trade unions and people within trade unions have exercised their power over the years to prevent the necessary rationalisations of industry; to prevent people from exercising their sovereign 'right' within the market place to make money.

Power and powerlessness have manifested themselves in Britain through the mechanism of a class-based politics. In other words, politics in Britain is class-ridden, and has been all through the twentieth-century; and this class basis reaches its apogee in industrial politics. Some make the mistake of overemphasising class: sometimes socialists, for example, speak of the working class as if it is a homogeneous entity, held together by a great traditional loyalty; sometimes the business class is similarly spoken of as if it is homogeneous. Neither is the case. Workers have a great deal to think about other than class; different business people and groups often have conflicting interests. Nevertheless, the class-based nature of British politics cannot be overlooked. The two major political parties in Britain have class-based roots. Most of the major interest groups represent one class or other.

The problem which confronts governments is how to manage these interests so as to ensure industrial progress; and industrial progress is dependent upon industrial change. There will always be some interest group opposed to change, because change often means that one group loses out, albeit often temporarily, until the new economic environment is created. Some may remain dispossessed even then, but this does not detract from the central principle that industrial change is a necessity. Industrial change has to take place because products made with last year's, or the last hundred year's, tools are bound to be more expensive than products from competing economies. In addition, the nature of demand changes. People do not want the products of a hundred years, or even ten years, ago. Most people have a dual economic role in society: as workers of one sort or another, and as consumers. In their role as consumers, they will welcome modernising change and greater competition in the corporate sector, even if this occasionally conflicts with their interests as workers. It is in the interests of all domestic and industrial consumers to obtain electricity at the cheapest possible price; this may conflict, however, with the interests of certain communities to keep open so-called 'uneconomic' pits in order to provide jobs. The key question facing national governments is which mechanism of industrial change is to be employed. The free market, even if it provides for great disparities of personal wealth and power? Even if many fall by the wayside? Or government intervention, even if this means restricting certain people's freedom to invest where and when they want? If it means restricting people from importing and exporting their own money? It is not black and white, of course. A government could decide to mix intervention with the market and, in practice, that is what all of them have done, with different degrees of emphasis.

When the class-based nature of British politics inhibits industrial change, where that is modernising change, we are all the losers. The interest groups that represent the different classes have to be made aware of this, and act upon it, or they deserve to wither. Thus trade unions in the emerging industrial future must focus upon their relevance to members, be democratic, consult their membership on important issues, provide welfare benefits and even retraining for periodically redundant members. If the nature of the industry is changing, as it obviously is, trade unions need to change with it. In a world which is becoming smaller through communications and transport revolutions they need to co-operate with other interest groups, not least the management and owners of business, to promote modernising change.

This also means, however, that business must have a sense of responsibility towards its employees. For, like soldiers in a conscript army, workers who feel hard done by make the worst workers. It is in the interests of the business class itself to be good employers. If there was a need for a 'macho' management style, as exhibited say by British Coal or Rupert Murdoch at Wapping in the 1980s, one would hope that the need was a transitional one. Class antagonism, like other antagonisms, produces negative forces. One should not have to be an idealist to hope for a future of industrial co-operation, where education and hard work can bring progress for employees whatever their class background, and success for British companies wherever they try to sell their products.

After all the arguments have been distilled, there are only two central concepts left and one leads on from the other: the question of economic efficiency and the question of political philosophy. Economic efficiency is necessary to provide wealth for people, which may or may not mean jobs as well, and a wide choice of cheap and good-quality products and services for consumers. The only political philosophies worth giving any time to are those that place a high emphasis on freedom and the happiness of people within society. Economic efficiency at any other price, say at the price of a completely state-run and state-owned economy, or in a free-market system where grinding poverty co-exists alongside fabulous wealth, is probably not worth having.

Select Bibliography

Allen, V.L. (1981) *The Militancy of British Miners*, The Moor Press, Shipley

Alt, J.E. and Chrystal, K.A. (1983) *Political Economics*, Wheatsheaf, Brighton

Anderson, P. (1964) 'The Origins of the Present Crisis' in *New Left Review* Vol. 23, January–February 1964

——(1968) 'Components of the National Culture' in *New Left Review* Vol. 50, July–August 1968

Archbishop of Canterbury's Commission on Urban Priority Areas (1985) *Faith in the City*, Church House Publishing, London

Bacon, R. and Eltis, W. (1978) *Britain's Economic Problem: Too Few Producers*, 2nd Edition, Macmillan, London

Batstone, E., Gourlay, S., Levie, H. and Moore, R. (1987) *Union Structure and Strategy in the Face of Technical Change*, Basil Blackwell, London

Blackaby, F. (ed.) (1978) *De-Industrialisation*, Heinemann Educational, London

Brittan, S. (1975) *Second Thoughts on Full Employment*, Centre for Policy Studies, London

Camilleri, J.A. (1984) *The State and Nuclear Power: Conflict and Control in the Western World*, Wheatsheaf, Brighton

Carr, E.H. (1981) *The Twenty Years' Crisis, 1919–1939*, Macmillan, London

Carrington, J.C. and Edwards, G.T. (1979) *Financing Industrial*

Investment, Macmillan, London

Confederation of British Industry/City Task Force (1987) *Investing in Britain's Future*, CBI, London

Department of Trade and Industry (1988) Cmnd 278 *DTI—the Department for Enterprise*, HMSO, London

Edwardes, M. (1983) *Back from the Brink*, Collins, London

Fiddler, J. (1981) *The British Business Elite: Its Attitudes to Class, Status and Power*, Routledge & Kegan Paul, London

Friedman, M. and Friedman, R. (1980) *Free to Choose*, Harcourt, Brace, Jovanovitch, New York

Gamble, A. (1981) *Britain in Decline: Economic Policy, Political Strategy and the British State*, Macmillan, London

Gilmour, I. (1978) *Inside Right: A Study of Conservatism*, Hutchinson, London

——(1983) *Britain Can Work*, Martin Robertson, Oxford

Glyn, A. and Harrison, J. (1980) *The British Economic Disaster*, Pluto Press, London

Goodman G. (1985) *The Miners' Strike*, Pluto Press, London

Gorz, A. (1985) *Paths to Paradise: On the Liberation from Work*, Pluto Press, London

——(1986) *Farewell to the Working Class: An Essay on Post-Industrial Socialism*, Pluto Press, London

Grant, W. (1982) *The Political Economy of Industrial Policy*, Butterworths, London

Grant W. with Sargent, J. (1987) *Business and Politics in Britain*, Macmillan, London

Grant, W. and Nath, S. (1984) *The Politics of Economic Policymaking*, Basil Blackwell, Oxford

Hall, T. (1981) *King Coal: Miners, Coal and Britain's Industrial Future*, Penguin, Harmondsworth

——(1986) *Nuclear Politics: The History of Nuclear Power in Britain*, Penguin, Harmondsworth

Handy, C. (1984) *The Future of Work—A Guide to a Changing Society*, Basil Blackwell, Oxford

Hastings, S. and Levie, H. (1983) *Privatisation?*, Spokesman, Nottingham

Heald, D. and Steel, D. (1982) 'Privatising Public Enterprise: An Analysis of the Government's Case' in *Political Quarterly*, 53, No. 53, July–September 1982

Heineman, M. (1944) *Britain's Coal: A Study of the Mining Crisis*, Victor Gollancz, London

Holland, S. (1975) *The Socialist Challenge*, Quartet, London

——(1980) *UnCommon Market: Capital, Class and Power in the European Community*, Macmillan, London

Illich, I.D. (1973) *Tools for Conviviality*, Calder & Boyars, London

Jenkins, C. and Sherman, B. (1979) *The Collapse of Work*, Eyre Methuen, London

Jenkins, R. (1987) *Baldwin*, Collins, London

Kirk, G. (ed.) (1982) *Schumacher on Energy*, Jonathan Cape, London

Marx, K. and Engels, F. (1975) *The Communist Manifesto*, Progress Publishers, Moscow

Minns, R . (1982) *Take Over the City: The Case for Public Ownership of Financial Institutions*, Pluto Press, London

Mishan, E.J. (1967) *The Cost of Economic Growth*, Penguin, Harmondsworth

Oxford Review of Economic Policy Vol. 3, No. 4, Winter 1987

Pollard, S. (1982) *The Wasting of the British Economy*, Croom Helm, London

Powell, J.E. (1969) *Freedom and Reality* (ed. J. Wood), Elliot Rightway Books, Kingswood

Sainsbury D. (1981) *Government and Industry: A New Partnership*, Fabian Research Series 347

Scargill, A. and Khan, P. (1980) *The Myth of Workers' Control*, Occasional Papers, Universities of Leeds and Nottingham

Schumacher, E.F. (1973) *Small is Beautiful: A Study of Economics as if People Mattered*, Abacus, London

Skidelsky, R. (1983) *John Maynard Keynes, Volume 1: Hopes Betrayed 1883–1920*, Macmillan, London

Steel, D. and Heald, D. (eds.) (1984) *Privatizing Public Enterprises*, Royal Institute of Public Administration, London

Streek, W. (1984) *Industrial Relations in West Germany: A Case Study of the Car Industry*, Heinemann, London

Taylor, A. (1984) *The Politics of the Yorkshire Miners*, Croom Helm, London

Whitfield, D. (1983) *Making It Public: Evidence and Action Against Privatisation*, Pluto Press, London

Wiener, M. (1981) *English Culture and the Decline of the Industrial Spirit 1850–1980*, Cambridge University Press, Cambridge

Williams, K., Williams, J. and Thomas, D. (1983) *Why Are the British Bad at Manufacturing?*, Routledge & Kegan Paul, London

Wilson, H. (1971) *The Labour Government, 1964–1970: A Personal Record*, Weidenfeld & Nicolson and Michael Joseph, London

Young, K. and Mason, C. (eds) *Urban Economic Development: New Roles and Relationships*, Macmillan, London

Index